Doctrinal & Inspirational

"WHOM THE LORD LOVETH"

"WHOM THE LORD LOVETH"

A MANUAL OF COMFORT FOR THE TESTED AND TRIED

By

J. R. MILLER

ROD AND STAFF PUBLISHERS, INC.
Crockett, Kentucky 41413
Telephone (606) 522-4348

This edition is an extensive revision of *The Ministry of Comfort*, thirteenth printing, published in 1901 by T. Y. Crowell & Company.

For many readers the message will bring comfort in time of suffering, direction for a Scriptural response to mistreatment, and strength to bear the trials of life. Jesus Christ is held before the reader as the perfect example and the source of wisdom and strength.

Readers reading books that were published a century ago often find it difficult to understand the language in which they were written. An effort has been made to prepare this material in the language of the present day.

—*The Publishers*

Copyright 1996
ROD AND STAFF PUBLISHERS, INC.
Crockett, Kentucky   41413

Printed in U.S.A.
ISBN 0-7399-0205-9
Code no. 96-3-05
Catalog no. 2328

TABLE OF CONTENTS

Preface

1. The Secret of Happiness 11
2. Glimpses of Immortality 18
3. Why Trouble Comes 28
4. "But He for Our Profit . . ." 36
5. Love in Taking Away 47
6. Trouble as a Trust 56
7. Some Blessings of Sorrow 69
8. Comfort in God's Will 77
9. Jesus as a Comforter 87
10. God Himself the Best Comfort 97
11. The Duty of Forgetting Sorrow 105
12. Effectual Prayer 117

13. The Humbling of Self 129
14. Godly Character Refinement 135
15. The Secret of Serving 145
16. Thinking Soberly 153
17. Facing Disagreeable Situations 161
18. The Duty of Thanksgiving 169
19. "Charity Never Faileth" 177
20. Putting Away Childish Things 186

PREFACE

A minister should offer a word of comfort in every service in which he takes part. Every congregation, no matter how small, that assembles has in it at least one sorrowful person who will go away unhelped if the Scripture lesson, hymns, or prayers contain nothing to lift up his heavy heart.

No book for devotional reading would be complete either if it contained nothing for those who are in sorrow. In this book special prominence is given to the ministry of comfort in the hope that it may make some hearts braver and stronger in the hard and painful ways of life. It is affectionately dedicated to those who are called to pass through trial.

—J.R.M.
Philadelphia, U.S.A.

"Blessed be God, even the Father of our Lord Jesus Christ, the Father of mercies, and the God of all comfort; who comforteth us in all our tribulation, that we may be able to comfort them which are in any trouble, by the comfort wherewith we ourselves are comforted of God" (2 Corinthians 1:3, 4).

CHAPTER ONE

The Secret of Happiness

It is easy enough to be pleasant
  When life flows by like a song;
But the man worthwhile is the one who
    will smile
  When everything goes wrong.
For the test of the heart is trouble,
  And it always comes with years;
And the smile that is worth the praises
    of earth
  Is the smile that shines through tears.

"WHOM THE LORD LOVETH"

Every person is born with a carnal nature. This means that he is doomed to be a selfish, unhappy, sinful person, constantly at odds with himself and those around him, unless he can find a way to turn himself into someone new.

Happily for us, this is not as impossible as it sounds. God has made a way that we can be turned into someone new. The Bible tells us, **"Therefore if any man be in Christ, he is a new creature: old things are passed away; behold, all things are become new"** *(2 Corinthians 5:17)*.

To become a new creature, a person must be born again, as Jesus told Nicodemus, **"Except a man be born again, he cannot see the kingdom of God"** *(John 3:3)*. Nicodemus found this a very hard thing to understand. He could not see how a full-grown man could be born a second time! He did not realize that Jesus was talking about a spiritual rebirth, not a natural one.

Before a person can be born again, he must realize that he is a sinner. He is lost and without hope for this life and the next. He also needs to realize that all the good things he might do in his own strength will not be enough to save him. He is lost and doomed, and it is beyond his power to do anything about it, except one thing. He can cry to God in repentance, asking for mercy and pardon, and allow God to do His work of regeneration in him.

We have Christ's promise that everyone who comes to Him, **"[He] will in no wise cast out" (John 6:37).** God is willing to save anyone who truly repents of his sins and humbly begs for mercy.

When a person is born again, a number of things happen. God performs a marvelous miracle in him that is almost beyond our limited understanding. He gives the sinner a new nature, turning him into a new person with new desires.

The story is told of a very vile man who worked on the railroad. One day this man became ill. In the hospital he realized how sinful he was and called on God for deliverance. The Lord performed His miracle of grace in him and saved him. This changed his life so drastically that when he returned to his work, his old friends could hardly believe that he was the same person. He told them, "I died in the hospital. I am someone different than the man you knew before!"

So it is with all those who are born again. The Bible describes it like this: **"I am crucified with Christ: nevertheless I live; yet not I, but Christ liveth in me: and the life which I now live in the flesh I live by the faith of the Son of God, who loved me, and gave himself for me" (Galatians 2:20).**

When a person is born again, the Holy Spirit enters him. The Holy Spirit guides the Christian into all Truth. He gives him strength to live in victory over the sins that he once committed. It also provides a link between the Christian and God, through which we can communicate with God and He with us.

Even after the miracle that God has worked in us, it is possible for us to turn our backs on what has happened to us and return to the old life again. The Holy

The Secret of Happiness

Spirit is God's gift to us to keep us from being dragged back into our old life of sin. He will warn us when we start to drift away and, if we heed His warnings, will keep us from falling.

The person who is born again starts out with a clean slate. God has forgiven his past sins. He has received a new nature to make it possible for him to live in victory over sin in the future. He has the Holy Spirit to be his guide. Such a person possesses the key to the secret of happiness.

There is no greater happiness than the joy that comes into our hearts when God forgives our sins. But the story does not end there. Associated with the new life are some responsibilities. God expects that we will obey and serve Him in return for what He has done for us. We find many instructions in the Bible for Christians to follow. But we have to read the Bible if we want to know what they are, so it is essential that all Christians study the Bible. While we are not saved because of the things we do, we do obey God because we are saved. The person who refuses to follow the teachings of the Bible is disobeying God and cannot claim the promises that God gives to His children.

It is also very important that Christians become part of a church, a group of believers who practice the teachings of the Bible and help each member to be obedient to those teachings. Many of the Bible commands take for granted that the Christian is a part of such a group. We need the help of fellow believers to stay faithful to God.

When a person has the peace of Christ in his heart, he is not dependent on favorable circumstances or conditions to provide him with happiness. The apostle Paul said that he had learned to be content in whatever state he found himself. That is, he had a peace and joy in his heart that kept him from being discontented in any state or condition, whatever its discomforts were. We know that his circumstances were not always easy. But he sang songs in prison. He was always cheerful, not only when things went well but also when things went wrong.

There is no other unfailing secret of enduring happiness. Too many people are dependent upon external conditions—the house they live in, the people they are with, their food, their companions, the weather, their state of health, the comforts or discomforts of their circumstances. But when we have learned the secret of contentment, the things around us will not make us unhappy, no matter how unpleasant they may be.

CHAPTER TWO

Glimpses of Immortality

Even for the dead
I will not bind my soul to grief;
Death cannot long divide.
For is it not as though
The rose that climbed my garden wall
Has blossomed on the other side?
Death doth hide,
But not divide;
Thou art but on Christ's other side!
Thou art with Christ, and Christ with me;
In Christ united still are we.

The knowledge that we will live forever is a mighty motive in life. If we only think of what lies in the little dust circle about our feet, we miss the glory for which we were created. The realization that we are immortal gives a new meaning to every joy of life, to every hope of the heart, and to every work of our hands.

This realization is partly a matter of self-education. We must train ourselves to think of life from an eternal perspective. We should not allow our minds to dwell only on material things, keeping our eyes on the narrow patch of earth on which we walk. Instead, we must lift our thoughts to things that are unseen and eternal. This is very important in the truest religious training and discipline. We should grasp every opportunity to think of heavenly things.

"WHOM THE LORD LOVETH"

A literary friend tells of an experience with her eye doctor. Her eyes were troubling her, and she asked him if she did not need a pair of new glasses. After examining her eyes he replied that they needed rest, not different lenses. She assured him that this was impossible, due to her work. After a moment's thought, he asked her if she had some scenic views from her windows. She replied enthusiastically that she had. From her front porch she could see the Blue Ridge Mountains, and from her back window, the Allegheny foothills.

"That is just what you want," said the eye doctor. "When your eyes get tired from reading or writing, go stand at your back window or on your front porch, and look steadily at the mountains for five minutes—ten will be better. That far look will rest your eyes."

My friend found a parable for her spiritual life in these directions. When she tires of life's treadmill round of care and worry and conflicts with evil, she rests her eyes by getting a far vision. "Look up to the beauty of God's holiness," she tells herself. "Look up to the throngs of the redeemed, waiting inside heaven's gates. Think of eternity."

This is the outlook that the thought of eternal life gives us. We live in our narrow sphere in this world, treading round and round in the same little circle. Life's toils and tasks fill our hands so much that we scarcely have time to think of anything else. Our secular duties and the responsibility to earn our bread dim our vision of God and of heaven. We can rest the soul by lifting our eyes to eternity and remembering the great world that stretches away beyond the narrow horizons of time. The glimpses of eternity that we receive while we read the Bible or pray remind us that we are immortal and that life really has no horizon.

It is inspiring to realize that human life reaches out beyond death and into eternity. Dying is not the end; it is but another milestone in our lives. It is not a wall cutting off our path. It is a gate through which we pass into a fuller, better life. Here on earth we say we have but threescore and ten years to live, and must plan only for hopes or efforts that we can bring within this limit. But in eternity we may make plans that will require ten thousand years, for we shall never die.

Life on earth is short, even at the longest. We can do very little in our brief, broken years. Many times we begin things only to be interrupted in the middle of them, before we are half finished. God may call us to do something else or stop us by illness, or life may end, leaving the work unfinished. We need only to go into the office of a busy man whom God has suddenly called away and see the unfinished things he has left—a letter half written, a book half read, or a picture half done—to understand that life is full of mere fragments, mere beginnings of things.

If there is no life beyond death, our earthly lives have no meaning. However, the assurance of eternal life puts a new meaning into our lives now. The smallest things that we start in this world will have eternal consequences.

At the close of his chapter on the resurrection, the apostle Paul tells us that our labor is not in vain in the Lord. Beyond the narrow horizons of time, an eternal world awaits us. Nothing done for Christ here shall be in vain. All good things will live forever. Even our smallest actions may have eternal consequences.

There is comfort in this for those whose lives seem a failure here—crushed like a trampled flower under the heel of oppression, broken and torn by the tyranny of evil. There will be time in eternity for such broken lives to show their loveliness. Think of living a thousand years, a million years, in a world where there shall be no sin, no struggle, no injustice, no failure, but where every influence will be inspiring and enriching.

The truth of immortality also gives us a glimpse of those who have passed away before us into eternity. We miss them and we ask a thousand questions about them, but this world's wisdom has no answers for us. But seeing in God's Word Christ's glorious resurrection, we glimpse the green fields of heaven on the other side of death, and the saints rejoicing by the throne of God.

For example, think of the many mothers whose little children Death has taken! The bud did not have time to open during its short summer on earth. Death carried

"WHOM THE LORD LOVETH"

it away with all its potential of loveliness, power, and life. We weep in sorrow over our shattered hopes, but our faith in eternal life removes much of the sting of death. There will be time enough in heaven's long summer to enjoy its loveliness. The truth of eternal life lifts the veil of our mourning because we know we will see those sweet infant faces again in heaven.

> I wonder, oh, I wonder,
>   Where the little faces go,
> That come and smile and stay awhile,
>   And pass like flakes of snow—
> The dear, wee baby faces that
>   The world has never known,
> But mothers hide, so tender-eyed,
>   Deep in their hearts alone.
>
> I love to think that somewhere
>   In the country we call heaven,
> The land most fair of everywhere
>   Will unto them be given:
> A land of little faces—
>   Very little, very fair—
> And everyone shall know her own
>   And cleave unto it there.

Oh, grant it, loving Father,
   To the broken hearts that plead!
Thy way is best—yet, oh, to rest
   In perfect faith indeed!
To know that we shall find them,
   Even them, the wee ones dead,
At Thy right hand, in Thy bright land,
   By living waters led!

Only yesterday an anxious friend asked me some questions about those who have died. Are they sleeping or conscious? Do they love and remember us in glory? Are they greatly changed? When we find them again, will we know them?

The New Testament teaching about death and immortality would seem to answer these questions. It shows us Jesus Himself beyond death, and He was not sleeping or changed. He had the same gentle heart. He had not forgotten His friends. Surely it is the same with our dear ones who have passed from our sight. Death did not take their beauty from them but has enhanced it. It ended nothing in them that was worthwhile but has perfected them instead. The traits that we loved here are still theirs but

"WHOM THE LORD LOVETH"

more pure than before. We shall find them again and many others with them, and then we shall enjoy more perfectly the sweet life of love that began so happily here. George Klingle puts it beautifully thus:

> We are quite sure
> That God will give them back—
>   Bright, pure, and beautiful.
> We know He will but keep
> Our own and His
>   Until we fall asleep.
> We know He does not mean
> To break the strands reaching between
>   The here and there.
> He does not mean—though heaven be fair—
> To change the spirits entering there,
>   That they forget the eyes upraised and wet,
> The lips too still for prayer,
> The mute despair.
>   He will not take
> The spirits which He gave
> And make the glorified so new
>   That they are lost to me and you.

Thus it is that looking through the window of Christ's rent tomb we have a vision of life as immortal; and in the truth of immortality, we find boundless inspiration, comfort for every sorrow, and gain for every loss.

CHAPTER THREE

Why Trouble Comes

There is never a day so misty and gray
 That the blue is not somewhere above it;
There is never a mountaintop ever so bleak,
 That some little flower does not love it.

There is never a night so dreary and dark
 That the stars are not somewhere shining;
There is never a cloud so heavy and black
 That it has not a silver lining.

Why Trouble Comes

There is always a mystery in sorrow. We often ask questions when we find ourselves in the midst of trouble. But many of our questions must remain unanswered until earth's dim light becomes full and clear in heaven's glory. **"What I do thou knowest not now,"** said the Master, **"but thou shalt know hereafter" (John 13:7).**

When trouble comes upon some Christians, they are afraid that they have displeased God in some way and that He is punishing them for it. This was the thought in the minds of the disciples when they asked Jesus whether a certain man had been born blind for his sin or his parents'. Jesus answered that God had not sent the blindness because of anyone's sin, but to give Him an opportunity to reveal His mercy and gentleness. When we have sorrow or suffering, our question should not be "What have I done to cause God to punish me?" but "What is the mission of this messenger of God to me?"

When we greet pain or trouble in this way, and welcome it reverently in Christ's Name, we are ready to receive whatever blessing God has for us in it. Whatever trouble comes to us comes from God on an errand of love. It is not some chance thing breaking into our lives, without purpose or intention. It is a messenger from God and brings blessings to us. Our trouble is God's gift to us. No matter what it may be—duty, responsibility, struggle, pain, unrequited service, unjust treatment, hard conditions—it is that which God has given to us. No matter through whose fault it may seem to have come upon us, when the trouble is ours, it is a gift of God to us. And, being a gift from God, we may be sure that it has a divine blessing included with it. It may have a stern appearance; it may seem unkind, or even cruel, but, folded up in its forbidding form, it carries a treasure of mercy. Even though troubles do not always originate with God, as in Job's case, we never have any troubles that God has not allowed to

Why Trouble Comes

come upon us for some good reason.

It is easy to find illustrations of this truth. The world's greatest blessings have come out of its greatest sorrows. Goethe said, "I never had an affliction which did not turn into a poem." No doubt many of the best hymns and poems had a similar origin, if we could know the story behind them. It is universally true that poets "learn in suffering what they teach in song." Nothing really worthwhile in life's lessons comes without pain and cost.

When we read a Christian book, we will find words of encouragement to cheer and strengthen us, and help us to be better Christians. But most of us do not realize what it cost the writer to prepare these words. We do not see how he suffered, struggled, and endured to learn to write the sentences that help us, and what struggles he went through to learn the lessons that he is portraying for us. One of the rewards of suffering is the power to light the way for other sufferers.

Some of the world's greatest blessings have been the fruit of a bitter sorrow or a loss that seemed overwhelming. When Mr. Moon of Brighton was at the zenith of his powers and the summit of his achievements, he became totally blind. It seemed a terrible calamity that a man so brilliant and helpful to humanity should have his career of usefulness so ruthlessly ended. For a time his heart was full of rebellious thoughts; he could not and would not submit. He could not see any good reason for the blindness that had ended his career.

In his darkness, however, he began to think of others who were blind and to wonder whether there might not be some way to help them to read. The outcome of his thought was the invention of the alphabet for the blind, which is now used in nearly every country and language. Because of his calamity, three or four million blind people in all parts of the world can now read the Bible and other books. Was it not worthwhile for one man's eyes to be darkened so that such a gift might be given to the blind of all lands?

Sorrows often give birth to blessings and joys in our lives. Many a man has set his heart on the things of earth only to have to give them up so that his affections may be lifted to heavenly and eternal things. There are many people who never

Why Trouble Comes

saw Christ until the human beauty that was blocking their vision faded before their eyes. Then, looking up in the darkness, they saw His face beaming its love upon them.

Through the clouded glass
Of our own bitter tears we learn to look
Undazzled on the kindness of God's face.
Earth is too dark, and heaven alone shines through.

A writer tells of a little bird that would not learn the song its master wanted it to sing. It listened to the other birds around it and learned snatches of their songs but never a separate and entire melody of its own. Finally the master placed its cage in a dark room by itself. Here the little bird learned to listen to the song that God had placed within its breast and to sing it. When it had caught the melody, the master brought the cage out into the light again. From then on it sweetly sang its own song.

Too many of us are like this little bird. Our Master has a song He wishes to teach us, but we will not learn it. The music of earth is so thrilling to us that we get only

"WHOM THE LORD LOVETH"

a note here and there of the song God has for us. So the Master makes it dark about us and calls us aside to suffer, hoping that we will give heed to the song He wants to teach us. When we have finally learned it to His satisfaction in darkness, He brings us back into the light to share it wherever we go.

> The clouds which rise with thunder slake
>   Our thirsty souls with rain;
> The blow most dreaded falls to break
>   From off our limbs a chain;
> And wrongs of man to man but make
>   The love of God more plain
>
> As through the shadowy lens of even
> The eye looks farthest into heaven
>   On gleams of star and depths of blue
>   The glaring sunshine never knew.

When we begin to realize that troubles are bearers of God's best blessings to us, we will not fear them as we did before. They do not break into our life without God's permission. They do not come laden with hurt; they come as God's servants, and they bear divine blessings in their hands. They do not come as avenging messengers to inflict punishment, but as angels of love to chasten us. They will help to cure us of follies and sins and lead us nearer to God, bringing out more of the beauty of Christ in us. Every trouble that ever comes to us brings us a blessing if we will accept it.

But we must welcome these divine messengers reverently the way men such as Abraham received and entertained the angels who came to their doors. Too often we refuse to accept sorrow's gifts and do not welcome God's messengers. Then we lose the blessings that God had intended for us to enjoy.

It is a serious thing to refuse to welcome troubles that God has sent to us. We turn Christ Himself from our doors when we refuse what He sends to us, though it be a sorrow or a loss. We thrust away heavenly treasures, shutting our hearts against them. We must open our doors to trouble as coming from God on an errand of love, its hands filled with priceless gifts to enrich us.

CHAPTER FOUR

"But He for Our Profit . . . "

I have no answer of myself for thee,
Save what I learned beside my mother's knee:
All is of God that is, and is to be;
   And God is good. Let this suffice us still,
   Resting in childlike trust upon His will
   Who moves to His great ends unthwarted
      by the ill.

"But He for Our Profit . . ."

Chastening is always painful, but we know that it is for our good. It corrects things in us that are wrong, and brings out qualities of divine beauty in us that otherwise would not be developed.

The writer of the Epistle to the Hebrews reminds us that we are God's sons. He admonishes us to heed the chastening of the Lord and not faint when He reproves us: **"For whom the Lord loveth he chasteneth, and scourgeth every son whom he receiveth. . . . God dealeth with you as with sons" (Hebrews 12:6, 7).**

Referring to our acceptance of the chastening of earthly parents, he says: **"Furthermore we have had fathers of our flesh which corrected us, and we gave them reverence: shall we not much rather be in subjection unto the Father of spirits, and live? For they verily for a few days** chastened us after their own pleasure; but he for our profit, that we might be partakers of his holiness" (Hebrews 12:9, 10). The wisest and most loving earthly father may not always chasten either wisely or lovingly, but every chastening our heavenly Father administers is for our good.

The next verse interprets the purpose of the trials that God sends into our lives: "**Now no chastening for the present seemeth to be joyous, but grievous: nevertheless afterward it yieldeth the peaceable fruit of righteousness unto them which are exercised thereby**" (Hebrews 12:11).

The teaching is clear and positive. Even though chastening is painful, we know that it is good for us. We do not know how much we owe to suffering. Many of the richest blessings that have come down to us from the past are the fruit of sorrow or pain. Others sowed in tears, and we gather the harvest in joy. We should never forget that redemption, the world's greatest blessing, is the fruit of the world's greatest sorrow. All chastening designed by our Father is for our profit, and if we receive it gratefully and endure it patiently, it will yield the fruit of righteousness in our lives.

Jesus uses the process of pruning to illustrate one form of God's chastening. In John 15:1, 2, He says, **"I am the true vine, and my Father is the husbandman. Every branch in me that beareth not fruit he taketh away: and every branch that beareth fruit, he purgeth it, that it may bring forth more fruit."** These verses contain much comfort for us during the time the knife is doing its painful work.

First, they tell us that the Father is the husbandman. We know that our Father loves us and would never do anything unloving or harmful to us. He is infinitely wise, planning our lives far in advance. His plan is the best for us, not only for today, but also for the future. When we need sharp pruning, when the knife cuts deep and the pain is sore, it is an unspeakable comfort to read, **"My Father is the husbandman."**

Second, it is inspiring to notice that it is the fruitful branch that the Father prunes. Sometimes when God leads Christians through trials they feel like saying, "Surely God does not love me, or He would not afflict me so sorely." But when we read the Master's words **"Every branch that beareth fruit, he purgeth,"** these distressing thoughts about our troubles somehow lessen. It is not punishment to which we are being subjected, but pruning, and we are being pruned because we are fruitful.

A third comfort is revealed in the purpose of the pruning: **"That it may bring forth more fruit."** The purpose of God's pruning is always fruitfulness. If a person who does not understand the process of pruning sees a man cutting away branch after branch of a tree or vine, it might seem destructive to him. But those who understand the object of the pruning know that what the gardener is doing will add to the value of the vine and to its ultimate fruitfulness. So it is with God's pruning in our lives as well.

Marvin R. Vincent tells of being in a great hothouse where luscious clusters of grapes were hanging from vines on every side. The owner told him, "When my new gardener came, he said he would have nothing to do with these vines unless he could cut them clean down to the stalk,

"But He for Our Profit . . ."

which he did. We had no grapes for two years, but this is the result."

There are some rich parallels between the natural pruning process and the spiritual pruning that God applies to our Christian lives. To the casual onlooker, the pruning seems to be destroying the vine. The gardener appears to be cutting it all away. But he sees into the future and knows that the vine will be richer and bear more fruit because of the pruning.

Every trouble that comes into the life of a believer brings some gift from God. There are some blessings that can be given only through pain and earthly loss, and some lessons that only suffering teaches. There are heavenly songs we can never learn to sing while we are enjoying earth's ease. We need the training God gives in His school of trial. In our short-sightedness we dread the hard things of life and try to escape the bitter cups it brings us. If only we knew it, these unwelcome experiences bring us rich gifts and benefits. There are some blessings we never can have unless we are ready to pay the price of pain. There is no other way to reach them.

"WHOM THE LORD LOVETH"

> God draws a cloud over each gleaming morn;
>   Would we ask why?
> It is because all noblest things are born
>   In agony.
> Only upon some cross of pain or woe
>   God's son may lie;
> Each soul redeemed from self and sin must know
>   Its Calvary.
> Yet we must crave neither for joy nor grief;
>   God chooses best:
> He only knows our sick soul's best relief
>   And gives us rest.

There is a common misconception regarding answers to prayer that would be corrected if we better understood the meaning of trouble. In our time of suffering or sorrow we cry to God for relief, asking Him to take away the trial that is so hard to endure. We forget that this trial is a messenger of good from God to us. When we ask our Father to free us from a painful experience, we are really asking Him to recall an angel of mercy who has come with rich gifts for us.

How should we pray in such a case? There is no harm in asking earnestly that the suffering may pass, but we should ask reverently, leaving it to God to decide what is best. In the Garden when Jesus faced the cross, He prayed, **"Father, if thou be willing, remove this cup from me: nevertheless not my will, but thine, be done" (Luke 22:42).**

Or the prayer should be that if He does not take away the trouble He would strengthen us to endure it, that we would not fail to receive its blessing. God does not promise to remove our burden or carry it for us. If there is a blessing in it for us, it would not be a kindness for Him to take it away before it has accomplished His purpose.

We have the assurance, however, that He will sustain us as we bear our load. This may disappoint the people who only turn to God with their trouble because they hope to get relief from it. But when we remember that God with a loving purpose has designed our trouble, we know we cannot afford to lose it. To be freed from it would be to miss the benefit that is in it for us.

We grow best under adversity. So in love and wisdom God leaves the load on our shoulders so that we may carry it and through it get the gift that He has sent us. He then gives us strength to bear it, strengthening us under its weight.

People often misunderstand the word *comfort*. Many persons looking for comfort in sorrow expect that God will take away the bitter cup, or at least make its bitterness easier to endure. But the word *comfort* comes from a root that means "to strengthen." Immediately after Jesus' prayer cited above, **"there appeared an angel unto him from heaven, strengthening him" (Luke 22:43).** To receive comfort is not a promise to make our burden lighter, or our grief less distressing. God comforts us by giving us strength to endure our trial.

For example, when wo turn to Him in grief because of the death of one we love, He does not bring them back to life for us. Nor does He make the loss appear less—which He could do only by making us love less, since love and grief grow on the same stalk. Rather, He gives us a new revelation of His own love to fill the emptiness. Into our hearts He puts new visions of the life into which our friend has gone to help us to rejoice in his happiness and glory.

"But He for Our Profit..."

The experience of Jesus in the Garden of Gethsemane is a good illustration of the way God comforts His own in times of trial. Jesus was human, and He dreaded the trial He was facing just as we dread the trials we face. He prayed for God to deliver Him from the experience He was facing, but it is also evident from His prayer that He was willing to go through it if God asked it of Him.

God did not answer His prayer in the way we might have expected. Instead of relieving Him of His suffering, God gave Him strength to bear it. In this way He received comfort and passed through His bitter trial on the cross without one cry of rebellion, His heart filled with perfect peace.

God usually comforts His people this way—not by removing their weight of sorrow or pain but by strengthening them to endure it in victory.

God's comfort can keep your heart sweet and unhurt in the midst of the sorest trials and bring your life through the darkest hours shining in transfigured beauty. Another author writes: "Strangely do some people talk of getting over a great sorrow—overleaping it, passing it by, thrusting it into oblivion. Not so. No one ever does that, at least no nature which can be touched by the feeling of grief at all. The only way is to pass through the ocean of affliction solemnly, slowly, with humility and faith, as the Israelites passed through the sea. Then its very waves of misery will divide and become to us a wall on the right side and on the left until the gulf narrows and narrows before our eyes and we land safe on the opposite shore."

CHAPTER FIVE

Love in Taking Away

Be strong, my soul!
Thy loved ones go within the veil.
God's thine, e'en so;
Be strong.

Be strong, my soul!
Death looms in view. Lo, here thy God!
He'll bear thee through;
Be strong.

"WHOM THE LORD LOVETH"

The account of Job is one of the finest examples of comfort in sorrow given us in the Scriptures. Job was a very rich man, but he lost almost everything he owned in a single day. Messengers came from every direction, one after the other, to tell him of troubles and losses. Then, last of all, he learned that a natural disaster had killed all his children. When he heard this, Job rent his garments, fell down upon the ground, and worshiped God. Instead of losing sight of God under the crushing blows that had fallen upon him, he turned at once to God, falling at His feet in reverence and homage. His faith did not fail. He had lost almost everything, yet in his grief and bereavement he said, *"The Lord gave, and the Lord hath taken away; blessed be the name of the Lord" (Job 1:21).*

It is easy enough to bless God for the

good things He does for us. God is always giving, and we readily see goodness and love in His gifts. It would have been easy for Job, as his prosperity increased, to say, "It is God who gives all this," and then to add, "Blessed be His holy Name." It would have been easy to praise God as, one by one, his children were born, bringing gladness and brightness into his home, and to say, "The Lord gave; blessed be the Name of the Lord."

But it was not so easy now, after all his prosperity had vanished, and his children taken, to say, **"The Lord gave, and the Lord hath taken away; blessed be the name of the Lord."** Yet that is just what Job did. It was the Lord who had given him all that had made his life happy, and it was the same Lord who now had taken everything away—the same Lord and the same love.

The calamities that fell upon the stricken father in such swift succession did not shake his trust. He was kept in perfect peace. He had received good at God's hands in countless ways, and he believed that God was still his friend even though he was experiencing trouble and disaster. He did not complain, nor blame God, but accepted the loss of his property and children with unquestioning confidence. The same Lord and the same love that had given them to him had now taken them away again.

There is immeasurable comfort in this truth for those whom God asks to return the gifts that He has bestowed upon them. God is a giving God, but He is also a God who sometimes takes away. Just because He takes something away from us, we should not feel that He has changed in His character or in His feeling toward us, His children. He loves us just as truly and as tenderly when He takes away that which we love as He did when He gave them to us. He sent them to us in love, for our good. When He takes them away, it is also in love, and for our good.

This is true, for example, of our friends. They are a blessing from God to us. We can say of them, "The Lord gave; blessed be the Name of the Lord." But, by and by, they are taken from us. One of every two friends must someday stand by the other's grave bearing an unshared grief. Will we be able to say, as Job did, "**The Lord hath**

taken away; blessed be the name of the Lord"? Can we believe that there is as true and holy love in the taking away as there was in the giving?

It is not necessary for us to understand why we need to experience loss or sorrow. It is here that faith comes in. We believe in God as our Father, and we trust His goodness, even when it takes from us all that we hold dear. Faith is that which asks no questions and does not need to know the reasons for God's ways. Often we cannot find reasons: God does not always show us why He does things.

Yet while we may not be able to fully understand, we may be able to see some elements of goodness in the taking away. For one thing, we know it is far more blessed and glorious for our friends in heaven than it ever could be here on earth. The sorest deprivation that could come to a Christian would be to never die. There are developments of life that can only be reached by dying. Our friends may have been happy here, and their life rich and beautiful, but we know that their life is fuller and richer where they are now, with Christ. True love is unselfish, and it ought to help reconcile us to our loss, knowing that our friends have entered eternal bliss. We ought to rejoice in their new happiness and in the honor that was shown to them by being received into heaven.

They are kept safe and secure for us in the home of God. We really have not lost them, although God has taken them out of our sight. They lose nothing of their beauty or their excellence of character in passing through death. The things that made them dear to us in this world will still be theirs when we meet them again. Indeed, they will have grown more beautiful and dear when we find them again.

When God takes our friends from us, we know that since God is love, He will compensate us for it in some way. Even the loss and the sorrow will work their ministry of good in us, unless we miss the blessing because of our attitude. It is possible for us to fail to get the good God sends by shutting our hearts against it. But there is no doubt that God gives us a gain in every loss. When He takes away one blessing He gives another. Perhaps the loss of the person we love makes more room in the heart for God Himself. Or the taking away of the strength that has meant so much to us trains us to lean more fully on Him, thus bringing out in us qualities that He wants to develop in us. The sorrow itself deepens our spiritual life and enriches our experience, giving us a new power of sympathy through which we may better comfort and help others.

Also, when our loved ones die, heaven becomes more real to us because they walk there now. A mother said it was easier for her to pray and think of Christ after her baby died, because she knew it was with Him. So, in many ways, new blessings come in place of those that have been taken away.

We know, too, that God never totally takes away from us any gift or blessing that He bestows. The flowers we love may fade, but if the flowers are in our hearts, they are ours forever. A picture that is lent to you for a little while may be removed, but while you remember its beauty none can take it from you. Your friend walked with you for a time, and then left you again; but the threads of his life are so

"WHOM THE LORD LOVETH"

deeply entangled with yours that you will never be really separated. Someday God will call us to come and be with Him too. Then we will meet them again.

> To give a thing and take again
> Is counted meanness among men;
> > To take away what once is given
> > Cannot then be the way of heaven!
>
> But human hearts are crumbly stuff,
> And never, never love enough;
> > Therefore God takes and, with a smile,
> > Puts our best things away awhile.
>
> Thereon some weep, some rave, some scorn,
> Some wish they never had been born;
> > Some humble grow at last and still,
> > And then God gives them what they will.

So it is only for a little while that God takes our loved ones from us. We shall meet them again, in their immortal beauty. He will keep them safe for us, and at length we will see them again, in radiant and imperishable loveliness. In this life we see only the beginnings of our good things—the bud and blossom. We will enjoy the full fruit when we enter the other and better life. One of the enjoyments of heaven will be renewing the friendships that death interrupted and making new ones.

> Let us hope on though the way be long
> And the darkness be gathering fast,
> For the turn in the road is a little way on
> Where the home lights will greet us at last.

CHAPTER SIX

Trouble as a Trust

Applauding crowds thy words may greet,
    Or marvel at the gift
That calls such music from the quiv'ring
    strings;
    But thou wilt never touch one heart
    Till thou hast felt its sufferings—or in part.

Then teach us, Son of God, to bear
    As Thou Thyself hast borne,
That from our deepest pain the power may
    spring
That makes our brother strong-
    The power of sympathy and love,
    Heav'n's richest dower.

Trouble as a Trust

A person wrote to a friend who had been a sufferer for some time, "God must love you very dearly to trust so much pain and sorrow to your care." The idea that God entrusts suffering to us is very thought-provoking. We do not normally think of it in this way. Yet there is no doubt that every trouble we have is really a trust committed to us to use as a gift of God and then to be accounted for.

Really, our entire life is a trust from God. Nothing that God gives us is for our use only. We do not receive our talent or talents to spend on ourselves or to use as we please. We must increase them by proper use in the service of the Master, and employ them for the benefit of the world. Then, someday, we will need to return them to our Lord when He calls for the accounting.

Money is a trust likewise: it is not our

"WHOM THE LORD LOVETH"

own but our Master's, to be used for Him in doing good to others. The same is true of all the blessings that we receive. We dare not use any of them selfishly; if we do they cease to be blessings to us. Even divine mercy, the greatest of all God's gifts, comes with the condition that we tell others about it and help them find it as well.

This is one of the laws of life. Everything God gives us, from the tiniest flower that blooms in our window to the infinite gift of eternal life, is entrusted to us that we may share it with those about us. It is bestowed upon us, not as a treasure to be hoarded but as a blessing to be dispensed. If we try to keep it just for ourselves, we will lose it. We can make its blessing our own only by using it for the good of others.

Suffering comes under the same law. It is a trust from God. It may have, and doubtless has, its peculiar meaning for us. But we must listen for its message so that we can speak it out again and others may hear it. It brings some gift of God expressly for us, but not for us to keep selfishly for ourselves. We must share with others the blessings we have received in our hours of need and trial so that they may be strengthened to face their struggles. In all trouble we are stewards of the mysteries of God.

Pain is a wonderful revealer. It teaches us many things that otherwise we never would have known. It opens windows through which we see, as never before, the beauty of God's love. But we must not hide these revelations in our hearts. If we try to keep them we shall miss their blessing. God has taught us these things so that we can share them with others. Then they can be a blessing for us and them.

God often calls His children to suffer so that they may honor God in some way. The life of Job illustrates this. Satan asked God with a sneer, **"Doth Job fear God for nought? Hast not thou made an hedge about him, and about his house, and about all that he hath on every side? thou hast blessed the work of his hands, and his substance is increased in the land. But put forth thine hand now, and touch all that he hath, and he will curse thee to thy face" (Job 1:9-11).**

God wanted to disprove Satan's challenge, so Job became the testing ground.

"WHOM THE LORD LOVETH"

He showed by his unshaken faith that he did not serve God for earthly reward but from true loyalty of soul.

Often Christians may be called to suffer for the sake of the witness they will give to the sincerity of their love for Christ and the reality of His divine grace in them. The world sneers at religious profession. It refuses to believe that it is genuine. It defiantly alleges that what we call Christian principle is only a cultural preference and that it will not stand severe testing. Then God calls good men to endure loss, suffering, or sorrow, not because they have any particular evil in their lives, but because the Master needs their witness to answer the sneers of the world.

This suggests how important it is for Christians to guard their witness carefully when they are passing through any trial. We never know how much depends upon the victory of our faith and joy in the hour of pain. Suppose that Job had failed, that he had not retained his integrity during his sore trial. Then Satan would have triumphed! But could it not be that our failure to be faithful and submissive during sickness, loss, or sorrow might bring grief to the heart of Christ and cause the adversary to reproach God's Name?

Even if the reason for our suffering may be unknown, we are never exempted from our duty of witnessing. Yet how many people think of this? We all understand that we are to confess Christ in our lives before men, in our conduct, our words, our disposition, our business, and our conflict with evil. But do we think of our duty to confess Christ in time of sorrow or trial? Too often those who seem loyal to Christ in all other experiences break down in trouble, their faith failing. There is no indication in the way they endure pain or loss to show that they are any different from those who are not Christians. The comforts of God and His Word do not appear to have any meaning for them. Instead of continuing to rejoice in the Lord, they grumble and complain or weep bitterly, just as does the person who does not know God.

But this is not how Christians should testify for their Master in their times of trial. Job's response was **"Blessed be the name of the Lord."** The divine promises cover every experience and provide the basis for the assurance of Christ's presence with us in every dark path and in every lonely way. The Bible clearly teaches us that the love of God never fails His children. It is as true and tender in times of affliction as it is in times of gladness, and it is the same when He takes away our blessings as it is when He gives them. **"We know that all things work together for good to them that love God" (Romans 8:28).** The Scriptures make it plain that no tribulation can harm us if we abide in Christ. He will preserve us through the most terrible trials if our faith does not fail.

Many of life's events are full of mystery; we cannot understand them, nor can we always see how they are consistent with God's love and wisdom. But we have the assurance that sometime we shall understand, and that in everything we shall see divine goodness.

With such comforts for every experience, no trial, however great, should ever cast us down. We should keep the divine promises of God in our hearts and believe them without question. We will still feel the pangs of grief—God will never blame us for our tears—but even in our deepest afflictions our faith should not fail and the songs of joy should not be choked. People are looking upon us and, consciously or unconsciously, watching to see what Christ can do for us in our sore distress. We must suffer victoriously to be a true witness for Him. With the help of God we can be more than conquerors through Him that loved us.

We say that we believe on Christ and in eternal life, but what does our believing do for us? Do we endure our trials in such a radiant way that we lead those who see us to believe in Christ and to seek His love and help for themselves? If we accept trouble as a trust, we will accept it reverently and submissively, and endure it patiently and sweetly. We will accept God's divine comfort and let it sustain and strengthen us so that we will pass through our times of trial singing and unhurt, with our life enriched. In this way our trouble will honor Christ and be a blessing to others.

God gave Abraham a greater test than most of us will ever face. He told him to take his only son, the son of his love and of promise, and offer him on an altar as a burnt offering. The record says that God

"WHOM THE LORD LOVETH"

gave this command to Abraham to prove him, to see if his faith would endure such a test.

Abraham did not disappoint Him. After it was all over, the angel of the Lord said to Abraham, **"Now I know that thou fearest God, . . . for because thou hast done this thing, and hast not withheld thy son, . . . in blessing I will bless thee"** (see Genesis 22:12–17). Abraham accepted his trial as a trust from God and was faithful. He did not fail God.

Who can tell what a blessing this account of Abraham's faithfulness has been to the world through the centuries? Abraham's example teaches other parents to give their children unquestioningly to God, willing that He should use them as He would, in whatever form of service would best honor Him and most greatly bless the world.

We are always in danger of becoming selfish during times of grief or sorrow. We are apt to forget our duty to those around us, thinking only of what we feel they should do for us. Some good people completely stop doing the tasks of love that once filled them with joy. They allow life

Trouble as a Trust

to become bitter, losing its sweetness, its joy, and its zest. Some people are never the same after a sore bereavement or a keen disappointment. They never regain their interest in others or their enthusiasm for duty. They come out of their trial self-centered and bitter, less ready for God to use.

But trouble will not affect us this way if we accept it as a trust from God. Not only will we endure it victoriously, sustained by Christ, but we can emerge from it ready for better service and for greater usefulness than ever before. We are told that Jesus was made perfect through suffering. Trouble prepares us for helping others in their troubles. Sorrow is a school, and when we learn its lessons it helps us to be a blessing in the world.

Our goal in life should not be to by-pass every pain or trial but to keep our heart sweet and our ministry of good uninterrupted throughout the trial, however hard or bitter it might be. The keenest suffering should only make us gentler in spirit and send us out to be even more loving and thoughtful than before—a blessing to everyone we meet.

"WHOM THE LORD LOVETH"

> Such a heart I'd bear in my bosom
>   That, treading the crowded street,
> My face should shed joy unlooked for
>   On every poor soul I meet;
> And such wisdom should crown my forehead
>   That, coming where counsels stand,
> I should carry the thoughts of justice
>   And establish the weal of the land.

The apostle Paul also taught that God gives us comfort as a trust. We do not receive it for ourselves only, but that we may give it out again to others. To the Corinthians he wrote in an outburst of joyous praise: **"Blessed be God, even the Father of our Lord Jesus Christ, the Father of mercies, and the God of all comfort; who comforteth us in all our tribulation, that we may be able to comfort them which are in any trouble, by the comfort wherewith we ourselves are comforted of God" (2 Corinthians 1:3, 4).**

God ministers comfort to us, not merely to get us through the trial or to strengthen us to endure our pain or loss, but also to prepare us to comfort others. When we have learned to say, "Thy will be done," in some great trial, and have been given grace to rejoice in tribulation, we have a secret that we must tell others. We must go to others in grief or trial, sit down beside them, and share with them what God did for us and giving them the words of God that have helped us.

We should pray for comfort in sorrow with this motive, that we may get a new blessing to take to others. It is selfish to ask for comfort merely that we may be able to endure our own pain or grief. But when we pray that God would teach us the lessons of comfort so that we may teach them again to others, our prayer pleases Him and He will answer our prayer. He will help us to overcome so that we may help others to be victorious.

Our lesson can be summarized into this: We are **"stewards of the mysteries of God. . . . It is required in stewards, that a man be found faithful" (1 Corinthians 4:1, 2).** When God sends us pain or sorrow, we are to be faithful. We are to accept our trust with love and to think of it as something that God has committed to us. However heavy the burden, it is a gift from God and has a blessing in it for us. We must treat it reverently and get from it whatever good God has sent to us in it. Then we must think of it also as something that we are to share with others.

It is a law among physicians that when one person makes a new discovery in medical science, he must share it with the whole profession, so that all may use the new knowledge. It should be a law of Christian life that every revelation, lesson, or blessing we receive from God we should use to help others in the Name of Christ.

> Oh, strengthen me, that while I stand
>   Firm on the Rock and strong in Thee,
> I may stretch out a loving hand
>   To wrestlers with the troubled sea.
>
> Oh, teach me, Lord, that I may teach
>   The precious things Thou dost impart;
> And wing my words, that they may reach
>   The hidden depths of many a heart.
>
> Oh, give Thine own sweet rest to me,
>   That I may speak with soothing power
> A word in season, as from Thee,
>   To weary ones in needful hour.

CHAPTER SEVEN

Some Blessings of Sorrow

The clouds which rise with thunder slake
    Our thirsty souls with rain;
The blow most dreaded falls to break
    From off our limbs a chain;
And wrongs of man to man but make
    The love of God more plain

As through the shadowy lens of even
The eye looks farthest into heaven
    On gleams of star and depths of blue
    The glaring sunshine never knew.

"WHOM THE LORD LOVETH"

It may seem strange to speak of the blessings of sorrow. At first thought we would say, "Surely nothing good can come from anything so terrible." Yet the Word of God and the experience of His people both teach us that many of the best blessings of life come out of affliction.

On the isle of Patmos, the apostle John had a vision of a glorified company honored above all the other saints in heaven. They wore white robes, carried palms in their hands, and stood nearest the throne and the Lamb. They looked as if they had never known a care or a grief. But when the question was asked, **"What are these which are arrayed in white robes? and whence came they?"** the answer was **"These are they which came out of great tribulation"** (Revelation 7:13, 14). They were the children of earth's sorrow. They had been taught in the school of trial.

Some Blessings of Sorrow

This vision would seem to indicate that those redeemed ones who have had the most affliction on earth attain the highest honor in heaven. Their robes are whitest, indicating surpassing purity. They bear palm branches as emblems of victory, showing that they have overcome in life's struggles. Of all the glorified, they are the nearest to Christ, verifying the promise, **"If we suffer, we shall also reign with him" (2 Timothy 2:12).**

This glimpse within heaven's gates confirms the Scriptures. The Bible tells us, **"We must through much tribulation enter into the kingdom of God" (Acts 14:22).** The way into a life of spiritual blessedness is through pain.

In the messages of Christ to the seven churches, in the first three chapters of Revelation, we see some of the blessings that Jesus promised to His followers. But these heavenly prizes will not be ours without a struggle. If we want to win them we must first fight the battle and be a victor. Every promise is prefaced with the condition **"To him that overcometh."** If we fail to overcome, we will miss the prize.

We do not know what we owe to our

sorrows. Without them we should miss the sweetest joys and the deepest experiences of life. Afflictions are opportunities. They come to us bearing blessings. If we refuse to accept our trials as God's plan of love for us, we will miss the blessings and be poorer all the rest of our days.

Pain helps to develop a person's character. Many a Christian endures a trial to emerge from the experience a better person, with his spirit softened, mellowed, and enriched, to be even more Christlike than before.

A photographer develops his film in a darkened room. He knows that the light of the sun on the film would mar the negatives. Even so there are features of spiritual beauty that cannot be produced in a life in the glare of human joy and prosperity. God brings out in many a soul its loveliest qualities by drawing the curtain and shutting out the light of human joy.

Sanctified afflictions soften the harshness of life. They tame the wildness of nature and consume the dross of selfishness and worldliness. They humble pride. They temper human ambitions. They quell fierce passions. They point out any traces

Some Blessings of Sorrow

of evil in our hearts; reveal our weaknesses, faults, and blemishes; and make us aware of our spiritual danger. They discipline the wayward spirit.

Sorrow draws its sharp plowshare through the heart, cutting deep, long furrows; and the heavenly Sower follows with the seeds of life. Then by and by fruits of righteousness spring up.

Sorrow has a humanizing influence. It makes us gentle and kindly toward each other. In no other school do our hearts learn the lessons of patience, tolerance, and forbearance so quickly as in the school of suffering. Love softens our harsh feelings and replaces our resentment. Many a household has been saved from disintegration by a grief that bows all hearts before God and wakes up the slumbering affections.

Often sorrow is one of the secrets of happy home life. It is a new marriage when young parents stand, side by side, by the coffin of their first-born. Grief is like a sacrament to those who share it with Christ beside them. Sorrow has cured many careless parents of their harshness of spirit and sharpness of speech, saving them from pride, coldness, and heedlessness. Most of us need the chastening of pain to bring out the best of our love.

Many people have found salvation because of a trial they had to endure. It was in his great distress that the prodigal **"came to himself"** *(Luke 15:17).* Many people seem to walk in a dream until some trouble arouses them. They are happy in their earthly gladness and satisfied with their human ambitions. They are blissfully unaware of the fleeting nature of this world and of the reality of eternity. They continue living in their dream until sorrow breaks in upon them. Perhaps some person who is very dear to them dies. In their grief they may see how perilous their spiritual condition is.

The story is told of a company of tourists on the Alps who were overtaken by night during a hike. After groping in the deep darkness for a time, they finally decided to settle down and wait until morning. A thunderstorm arose during the darkness, and a vivid lightning flash showed them that they had stopped on the very edge of a precipice. Only one more step forward and they would have fallen to their death. The lightning flashes of sorrow often reveal to people the peril in which they are living, and lead them to turn to God. Many redeemed ones in glory will look back to a great grief as the time of their salvation.

When we accept sorrow it will also prepare us to be better messengers of God to others. The apostle Paul tells us that the reason God comforts us in our trouble is so that we may become comforters of others in their afflictions. We have a new power with which to bless others when we have come from an experience of grief. A surrendered, caring heart is a wonderful interpreter of others' bereavements.

The power to help those who are in trouble, by binding up their broken hearts, is the most divine of all abilities. Surely, then, it is worthwhile to pay any price of pain or suffering to receive the divine anointing for such sacred ministry.

True comfort has a strange power to heal, to bind up broken hearts, and to turn sorrow into joy. The Christian home that is broken by death can have a deeper happiness than it ever had before, under

"WHOM THE LORD LOVETH"

the gentle influences of the divine love of Christ.

> "But I would not have you to be ignorant, brethren, concerning them which are asleep, that ye sorrow not, even as others which have no hope. For if we believe that Jesus died and rose again, even so them also which sleep in Jesus will God bring with him. . . . Then we which are alive and remain shall be caught up together with them in the clouds, to meet the Lord in the air: and so shall we ever be with the Lord. Wherefore comfort one another with these words."
> 1 Thessalonians 4:13, 14, 17, 18

CHAPTER EIGHT

Comfort in God's Will

Almighty, though I am dust,
Yet spirit am I, so I trust.
    Let come what may of life or death,
    I trust Thee with my sinking breath.
I trust Thee, though I see Thee not
In heaven or earth or any spot.
    I trust Thee till I shall know why
    There's one to live and one to die.
I trust Thee till Thyself shall prove
Thee Lord of life and death and love.
              —*Elizabeth Stuart Phelps*
              —*Adapted*

"WHOM THE LORD LOVETH"

A great secret of comfort lies in "Not my will but thine." When we can say this and abandon ourselves into God's hands, His peace will rule our hearts in quietness and confidence. The experience of Jesus in Gethsemane is a good illustration of this. There He faced the most terrible experience any soul ever met in this world—so terrible that He pleaded with God to allow Him to sidestep it. But, along with the plea for deliverance, He also prayed in submission, **"Not my will, but thine, be done" (Luke 22:42).** There was something more important to Him than the granting of His request: it was that nothing should hinder God's plan for man's redemption.

It is interesting to trace the course of the Gethsemane prayer from struggle to quiet surrender and perfect peace. The first supplication was **"O my Father, if it** be possible, let this cup pass from me: nevertheless not as I will, but as thou wilt."** A little later Jesus returned again to His prayer with the petition **"O my Father, if this cup may not pass away from me, except I drink it, thy will be done" (Matthew 26:39, 42).** His spirit of submission to God mastered the fierceness of the struggle in His soul. Finally, the agony was over. He had won the victory.

A little later, we have an echo of the comfort filling the heart of Jesus in His words to Peter when he had drawn his sword to resist the arrest of his Master. **"The cup which my Father hath given me, shall I not drink it?" (John 18:11).** There was no word of desire now for the passing away of the cup. Jesus had submitted to His Father's will and received comfort.

There is no other way by which true comfort can come to any heart in time of sorrow but by quiet submission. So long as we cannot say, **"Not my will, but thine, be done,"** the struggle is still going on, and we are still uncomforted. Comfort is peace, and there is no peace until there is submission to the will of God. If we want God's comfort, we must bring our wills into complete submission to His will.

There are many reasons for submitting to God's will. One is that God has a plan and a purpose for our lives. He knows what He wants to make of us and what He would have us do. Only He can disclose His plan for each particular life. Every time we resist His will and refuse any part of it, we mar God's plan. God's plan for us includes whatever sorrows or sufferings that may be necessary to bring out His image in us. Only by submission to His divine will can we have our lives fashioned after this heavenly pattern.

Another reason we should accept God's will in our lives without resistance or complaint is that God is our King and has a sovereign right to reign over us. Resisting His will is rebellion. Not only should our submission be complete, without condition and without reserve, in the smallest as well as in the greatest matters; it should also be cheerful and willing. Chafing and murmuring grieves God. We must accept the will of God with delight whether in duty or sorrow. This is the only way we can please God and have His benediction of peace.

Another reason for submitting to the divine will in time of trouble is that God always seeks our good. He is our Father and would never send anything into our lives that would harm us, nor take anything from us that would take away a blessing.

His wisdom is perfect, and He always knows what is best for us. We do not understand ourselves well enough to know this. We cannot predict what influence certain circumstances will have in our lives, nor can we know where a course would lead us. We have no wisdom to choose our lot, and we should always let God decide for us what is best.

> I would not dare, though it were offered me,
> To plan my lot for but a single day,
> So sure am I that all my life would be
> Marked with a blot in token of my sway.

The things we are so eager to get may do irreparable hurt to our spiritual lives. The blessing that we think is so indispensable to our happiness has perhaps done its work in us and needs to be taken away. God knows what is best for us, and

"WHOM THE LORD LOVETH"

His will is perfect wisdom and love. To resist it is to harm ourselves; to reject it and insist upon having our way is to choose evil for ourselves.

It is hard for us to believe that sorrow can bring us blessing. Yet there is no doubt that every grief or pain that comes to us brings us a blessing. God's gifts are always good. To refuse to accept a burden He would give us is to reject a gift of love from Him and to thrust away a blessing sent for our enrichment.

A diamond may sometimes be found in the heart of a rough stone. It is said that the first discovery of diamonds in South Africa was in some pebbles by the side of a road. A scientist came upon a group of boys using some of these stones for marbles. His keen eye detected the gem wrapped up in them. Similarly, our sorrows conceal the diamonds of God's love and grace within their forbidding exterior. We do not know how we are robbing ourselves when we refuse to accept the trials that come to us in God's providence. By submitting to the divine will we accept the good that our Father offers us.

There are those whom God calls to long

years of suffering or sorrow. It is a comfort for such to think of their pain or grief as a friend sent to accompany them on the way. Mrs. Gilchrist wrote of Mary Lamb, "She had a lifelong sorrow and learned to find its companionship sweet." When the sufferer learns to think like this of pain or sorrow, its bitterness turns to sweetness and his life finds blessing and inspiration in the sacred companionship.

When first I looked upon the face of Pain,
    I shrank repelled, as one shrinks from a foe
    Who stands with dagger poised, as for a blow.
I was in search of Pleasure and of Gain:
I turned aside to let him pass—in vain.
    He looked straight in my eyes and would not go.
    "Shake hands," he said. "Our paths are one,
        and so
We must be comrades on the way, 'tis plain."

I felt the firm clasp of his hand on mine;
    Through all my veins it sent a strengthening
        glow.
    I straightway linked my arm in his, and lo!
He led me forth to joys almost divine;
    With God's great truths enriched me in the end,
    And now I hold him as my dearest friend.

"WHOM THE LORD LOVETH"

It may be God's will to take something from us that we hold dear. God's love is the same whether He is giving us new blessings or taking away those we have had. The good things we enjoy are His, not ours. He has only lent them to us for a time and for a specific purpose. When their mission is finished, God recalls them, and we may be sure there is blessing in the recalling.

A beautiful story is told of a home with twin boys who were loved dearly by both of their parents. Both boys suddenly died while their father was absent. When the father returned, not knowing what had happened, the mother met him at the door and said, "I have had a strange visitor since you went away."

"Who was it?" asked the father with kindly interest.

"Five years ago," his wife answered, "a Friend lent me two precious jewels. Yesterday He came and asked me to return them to Him. What shall I do?"

"Are they His?" asked the father, not dreaming of her meaning.

"Yes, they belong to Him and were only lent to me."

Comfort in God's Will

"If they are His, He must have them again, if He desires."

Leading her husband to the boys' room, the wife drew down the sheet, uncovering the lovely forms, white as marble. "These are my jewels," said the mother. "Five years ago God lent them to me, and yesterday He came and asked them again. What shall we do?"

With a great sob, the father, bowing his head in submission, said, "The will of the Lord be done."

That is the way to find God's comfort. He has a right to take from us what He will, for all our joys and treasures belong to Him and are only lent to us for a time. It was in love that He gave them to us; it is in love that He takes them away. When we cease our struggle, and in faith and confidence submit our will to His, peace flows into our hearts and we receive comfort.

The secret of divine comfort is in completely and quietly yielding to the will of God. It does not make the sorrow less painful, or give back the departed loved one, but it brings the heart into full accord with God and gives us sweet peace. When we can say, "Not my will, but thine,"

"WHOM THE LORD LOVETH"

and mean it, we will stop struggling with our trials, and our souls will rest in undisturbed calm on the bosom of God. We still may not understand, but we will ask no more questions; we will simply trust and leave it all in our Father's hands, finding sweet comfort in Him.

> We see not; all our way
> 'Tis night; with Thee alone is day.
>> From out the torrent's troubled drift,
>> Above the storm our prayer we lift.
>>> Thy will be done!
> We take with solemn thankfulness
> Our burden up, nor ask it less;
>> And count it joy that even we
>> May suffer, serve, and wait for Thee.
>>> Thy will be done!

CHAPTER NINE

Jesus as a Comforter

And all through life I see a cross,
    Where sons of God yield up their breath;
There is no gain except by loss,
    There is no life except by death.

There is no vision save by faith,
    Nor glory but by bearing shame,
Nor justice but by taking blame.
    And that Eternal Passion saith,
Be emptied of glory, right, and name.
—W. Smith

"WHOM THE LORD LOVETH"

It is interesting to study Jesus as a comforter. He gave lasting comfort to His friends in their time of need. We have an illustration of this in the home of Mary and Martha. Their sorrow was very great because their brother, Lazarus, had died. Jesus came, not as their other friends had come, merely to mourn with them, but to bring comfort to their hearts in their overwhelming grief.

First, He gave them a glimpse of what lies beyond death. **"Thy brother shall rise again. . . . I am the resurrection, and the life: he that believeth in me, though he were dead, yet shall he live: and whosoever liveth and believeth in me shall never die"** *(John 11:23, 25, 26).* He opened a great window into the other world for them. It is a wonderful comfort for those who sorrow over the departure of a Christian friend, to know what the New Testament teaches

Jesus as a Comforer

about death. Death is not the end; it is a door that leads into fullness of life.

It is possible to believe the doctrine of the future resurrection but fail to get present comfort from it. When Jesus assured Martha that her brother would rise again, she said, **"I know that he shall rise again in the resurrection at the last day" (John 11:24)**. That hope seemed too distant to give her much comfort. Her sense of present loss outweighed every other thought and feeling. She wanted her brother back, and nothing else would bring any real comfort. Who that has stood by the grave of a precious friend has not experienced the same feeling Martha had?

The Master's reply of hope to Martha is revealing. To Martha, the resurrection was a dim, faraway consolation, but Jesus said, **"I am the resurrection."** In His mind, the resurrection was something present, not remote. He wanted to make plain to Martha this truth of eternal life. **"Whosoever liveth and believeth in me shall never die,"** He told her. The Christian does not die. Though the body dies, his soul lives on in eternity. The resurrection may be in the future, but there is no break whatever

"WHOM THE LORD LOVETH"

in the life of the believer in Christ. He has passed from our sight, but he still lives, thinks, feels, remembers, and loves in his eternal home.

>He hath solved the sacred mystery,
>   He hath crossed the great divide:
>Within the sacred city, far
>   Beyond the soundless tide,
>He the Master's face beholdeth,
>   Whom unseen we all adore.
>He now praises Him rejoicing
>   On that bright celestial shore.
>Praises be to God the Father,
>   We will live beyond the sky,
>Though, then folded like a garment,
>   We will lay our body by.
>Eternal life we then will enter,
>   By that full and swelling tide,
>Safe within the golden city,
>   Where the gates stand open wide.

This is a part of the comfort that Jesus gave to His friends in their bereavement. He assured them that for the believer there is no death. There remains, for those who stay behind, the pain of separation and of loneliness, but for those who

Jesus as a Comforer

have passed over we need have no fear.

How does Jesus comfort those left behind when death calls? We find the answer to this question in the story of the death of Lazarus, as well. You might say, "Of course Mary and Martha were comforted. He brought their brother back from the dead. He literally undid the work of death and grief in their family. If only He would do this for His followers now, they would be comforted too." But we must remember that the return of Lazarus to his home was only temporary. This was not a resurrection to eternal life; it was only a return to mortal life with all of its temptation, sickness, and pain. Lazarus would die again, and his sisters would experience the agony of separation and loneliness the second time, unless they died first. We can scarcely call this comfort—it was merely a postponement for a little while of the final separation.

But Jesus gave the sisters true comfort besides this, even before He raised Lazarus from the dead. His presence with them brought them comfort. They knew that He cared for them. Many times before, when He had come to their home,

"WHOM THE LORD LOVETH"

He had brought comfort. They felt secure and at peace in His presence. Their great grief was not as heart-rending because He was with them. Even human love has comforting power. It is easier to endure a sore trial if a trusted friend is beside us. But if Jesus is with him the believer can endure any sorrow.

Too often we do not realize that the Master is close beside us, and we miss the comfort of His love altogether. Several months later, Mary Magdelene stood by the empty grave of Jesus, broken-hearted, crying out for her Lord. He was close beside her, but she did not recognize Him, ***"supposing him to be the gardener" (John 20:15).*** A moment later, however, He spoke her name in the old familiar tone of voice, and instantly her sorrow turned into joy.

Even so we may stand in the deep shadows of grief, longing for comfort and love, while Christ is close beside us, closer than any human friend can be. If only we will look up into His face, believing, He will flood our souls with His wonderful love and swallow up our sorrows in fullness of joy. Christ is always present in our times of trouble; it is only because we remain

Jesus as a Comforer

unaware of His presence that it does not comfort us.

The sympathy of Jesus was another element of comfort for Mary and Martha. There was a wonderful gentleness in His manner as He received them. Mary's grief was deeper than Martha's. When Jesus saw her weeping, He groaned in the spirit and was troubled. Touched by her grief, He wept with her.

"Jesus wept" (John 11:35). It is a great comfort in time of sorrow to have human sympathy, to know that somebody cares and feels with us. It would have been a comfort for the sisters if John or Peter or James had wept with them beside their brother's grave. But the tears of the Master meant much more. They told of the holiest sympathy this world ever saw: the Son of God weeping with two sisters in a great human sorrow.

This verse reveals the heart of Jesus for all time. Wherever a believer in Christ is sorrowing, He stands by, unseen, sharing the grief. It is an immeasurable comfort to know that the Son of God suffers with us in our suffering and that He is touched with the feeling of our infirmities. We can

"WHOM THE LORD LOVETH"

endure our trouble more quietly when we know this.

Too often human sympathy is nothing but a sentiment. Our friends weep with us and then pass by on the other side. They tell us they are sorry for us, yet they do nothing to help us. But the sympathy of Jesus at Bethany was very practical. He came all the way from Peraea to be with them in their trouble. He showed His love by speaking words of divine comfort to them. He wept with them in their grief. Then He also wrought the greatest of all miracles to restore to them the joy of their hearts.

No doubt many Christians in the time of their bereavement have wished that Jesus would perform such a miracle for them. Many times He does what is in effect the same: in answer to the prayer of faith He spares the life of a dear one who seems about to die.

When we pray for the recovery of our friends who are sick, our prayer should always end with **"Not my will, but thine, be done."** We subdue even the most passionate longing of our affection in the quiet confidence of faith. If it is not best for our loved one for God to heal them, it would be selfish of us to demand it. It would not be a real blessing for us or them, if it is not God's way. If we pray seeking His will, we believe that the answer, whatever it may be, is God's best for us. When God takes away our loved ones, there is unspeakable comfort in the confidence that this was His will for them. If they recover, it is Christ who has given them back to us, as He gave back Lazarus to Martha and Mary.

The problem of sorrow in a Christian's life is a very serious one. We need a clear understanding of the subject so that we will not be robbed of our blessings when it falls to our lot to suffer. Every sorrow that comes to us brings something good from God. But we may reject the good and receive harm instead. There is in Jesus Christ an infinite resource of consolation, and we have only to open our hearts to receive it. Then He will sustain us in our sorrows by divine help and love, and we will come through the experience enriched in character and blessed in all of life.

Our griefs contain lessons for us to learn, and we should diligently seek to

"WHOM THE LORD LOVETH"

master whatever our Master would teach us. In every pain is folded the seed of a blessing; we must give the seed an opportunity to grow so that we may gather its fruit. A rainbow hides in every tear, but its splendor is revealed only when the sunshine falls upon it.

> The dark brown mold's upturned
>   By the sharp-pointed plow—
> And I've a lesson learned.
>
> My life is but a field,
>   Stretched out beneath God's sky,
> Some harvest rich to yield.
>
> Where grows the golden grain?
>   Where faith? Where sympathy?
> In a furrow cut by pain.

CHAPTER TEN

God Himself the Best Comfort

> My God, my God, let me for once look on Thee
> As though naught else existed, we alone;
> And as creation crumbles, my soul's spark
> Expands till I can say, even from myself,
> "I need Thee and I feel Thee and I love Thee."
> —*Browning*

"WHOM THE LORD LOVETH"

The most heart-satisfying comfort we can find in time of trouble is in God Himself and not in anything God says or does. It is a comfort to think of death as a process through which life passes from earth to heaven. The truth that man will live forever also gives comfort as we think of our departed friends entering into an existence of eternal joy. There is comfort, too, in the assurance that God makes no mistakes in any of His dealings with us and that sometime we shall see the beauty and good of our experience. We get a measure of comfort, also, in the divine assurance that **"all things work together for good to them that love God, to them who are the called according to his purpose" (Romans 8:28),** that sorrow has a mission, that within every trial God sends a blessing.

But the comfort that means most to the

bruised or broken heart is that which comes in personal communion with God. Too many people who claim to be Christians are satisfied with enjoying God's gifts and do not go on to develop a personal friendship with God Himself. God is better than His best gifts. It is always true that "the gift without the giver is bare." This is especially true of God and His gifts.

> O Lord, while show'ring on my path
>   Thy benedictions full and free,
> Whatever Thou givest, fail not Thou
>   To give of Thine own self to me.
> For dear as all Thy blessings are,
>   Thyself is more than all besides.
> This "Gift of gifts" alone I crave;
>   Bestow it, Lord, whate'er betides.
>   Come then what may,
>   By night or day,
> Through sunshine or through storm,
>   Safe in Thy care,
>   What need I fear?
> Naught, naught can do me harm.

There are many Christians who have found that a season of trial strengthened their relationship of personal friendship with God. During this time they found new treasures of love, of sympathy, and of comfort in Christ. When we seek for help in sorrow, we should look to the person of God, beyond the blessing of God, and even beyond the comfort we receive from His Word, to find satisfaction in our personal communion with Him.

God dispenses mercies and benefits on all of mankind. The Bible says, **"He maketh his sun to rise on the evil and on the good, and sendeth rain on the just and on the unjust" (Matthew 5:45).** But He desires to manifest Himself to His children in ways of which the world knows nothing. The Bible saints found their satisfaction and help in God Himself, not in His gifts. David did not say, **"I shall not want"** because he had great stores of God's gifts laid up, but because he knew the Lord was his shepherd. His confidence was not in the wealth that God had given him but in God Himself.

In Psalm 42:2 the writer is not longing for mere tokens of divine goodness or for benefits and favors when he cries out: **"My soul thirsteth for God, for the living God."** Only his fellowship with God could

God Himself the Best Comfort

quench his thirst. No gifts or blessings that God could have given him would have satisfied him. It was for God Himself that he thirsted. The human soul was made for God, and God alone can meet its need.

The only satisfying comfort, therefore, in time of sorrow is that which is in God Himself. He asks for our complete trust. Then He reveals Himself to us in the work of the Comforter, the Holy Spirit. Apart from this, there is no real comfort.

More than one Christian may look back to a godly home and say, "My mother's loving instinct was from God, and God was in her love to me. Through her example, I learned to love God, first for her sake and later for my own. She has been gone for years now, but her God stays by me still, embracing me in my old age as tenderly and carefully as Mother did when I was a baby. The greatest joy and principal glory of my life is that He helped me to become His child and allows me to call Him my Father."

That is a very beautiful thought. What the mother is to her baby, God is to His child unto the end. The Scriptures strive continually to make the truth of the divine nearness real to us. We call God our Father, but there is something about the mother's relation to her child that is even closer and more tender than a father's. So when God is earnestly seeking to make His people understand the tenderness of His love and yearning for them, He says, **"As one whom his mother comforteth, so will I comfort you"** *(Isaiah 66:13).*

> No word of all the Scripture
>   Thrills a sweeter chord than this,
> Stirs a richer retrospection
>   Of the soul's experienced bliss,
> Than this promise, where the Spirit
>   Strengthens weak and timid faith
> With assurance of His comfort,
>   As a mother comforteth.

Jesus took all His troubles straight to His Father. He spent much time in prayer, sometimes praying all night. He needed the strength of His Father's presence to endure the work He had called Him to do. In the Garden of Gethsemane, where He faced His greatest trial, He found rest in communing with God. His friends were no comfort to Him; they did not understand His struggle and slept while His soul was in bitter agony. But His communion with His Father gave Him the strength and courage to face the cross alone.

Our Master's example should be our guide in every experience of grief or trial. We appreciate the friends that offer words of comfort, and their presence in our sorrow. We are grateful for the verses of comfort in the Scriptures and in the assurance that our loving Father is in complete control of our trial. But the comfort that calms our spirits and brings comfort to our souls comes from our communion with God. We can share our deepest feelings with Him, and He will understand. He will not despise our tears. He knows how great our sorrow is and how hard it is for us to submit to it. But when we do, His presence with us will be a greater comfort than the comfort of all our other comforters combined.

Oh, the peace that floods our being at His touch! And the calmness that quiets our souls when He speaks! Do not pity the Christian in his trials; pity the person that tries to endure them in his own strength

"WHOM THE LORD LOVETH"

without allowing the comforting presence of God to heal him.

There is a blessing in true human sympathy. God sends our friends to us to bring us little measures of His own love—little cupfuls of His grace. But He Himself is the only true Comforter. His love alone is great enough to fill our hearts, and His hand alone has skill to bind up our wounds.

> **"Blessed be God, even the Father of our Lord Jesus Christ, the Father of mercies, and the God of all comfort; who comforteth us in all our tribulation, that we may be able to comfort them which are in any trouble, by the comfort wherewith we ourselves are comforted of God."**
> **2 Corinthians 1:3, 4**

CHAPTER ELEVEN

The Duty of Forgetting Sorrow

Thou knowest that through our tears
    Of hasty, selfish weeping
Comes surer sin, and for our petty fears
    Of loss Thou hast in keeping
A greater gain than all of which we dreamed;
    Thou knowest that in grasping
The bright possessions which so precious seemed
    We lose them; but if, clasping
Thy faithful hand, we tread with steadfast feet
    The path of Thy appointing,
There waits for us a treasury of sweet
    Delight, royal anointing
With oil of gladness and of strength.
               —*Helen Hunt Jackson*

"WHOM THE LORD LOVETH"

Sorrow leaves deep scars. We are never altogether the same after we have passed a deep sorrow.

There follows a mist and a weeping rain,
And life is never the same again.

In one sense we never forget sorrow. The old woman of ninety still remembers her grief of seventy years ago, when God took her first baby out of her bosom.

There is a proper way to remember grief. This kind of remembrance is not a mark of rebellion. Rather it brings rich blessing to the heart and life. Sorrow rightly accepted and cheerfully borne has a humanizing and fertilizing influence. "The memory of things precious keepeth warm the heart that once did hold them."

The recollections of losses, if sweetened by faith, hope, and love, are benedictions

The Duty of Forgetting Sorrow

to the lives they overshadow. The person who has never suffered is poorer than the one who has, because he has none of sorrow's marks upon him. But poorer yet is the person who has suffered and has forgotten the pain and does not bear in his life the beautifying traces of the experience of the sufferings through which he has passed, or has suppressed his memories so that they cannot have a continuing good influence upon him.

> We turn unblessed from faces fresh with beauty,
>   Unsoftened yet by fears,
> To those whose lines are chased by pain and duty
>   And know the touch of tears.
>
> The heart whose chords the gentle hand of sadness
>   Has touched in minor strain,
> Is filled with gracious joys, and knows a gladness
>   All others seek in vain.
>
> How poor a life where pathos tells no story,
>   Whose pathways reach no shrine,
> Which, free from suffering, misses too the glory
>   Of sympathies divine!

Yet there is a way of remembering sorrow that does not bring blessing or enrichment—that does not soften the heart or add beauty to the life. There is an unsubmissive remembering, a brooding over past losses and trials that makes us sad, bitter, and rebellious. Only evil can result from such memory of grief. We should not neglect our duties to turn aside and brood over our losses, constantly reliving them and refusing to allow the healing touch of God to work in us. We need to leave our griefs behind us while we go on reverently, faithfully, and quietly in our appointed way of duty.

There are many people, however, who have not learned this lesson. They live perpetually in the shadows of the trials and losses of their past. Nothing could be more unwholesome for our souls or more untrue to the spirit of Christian faith than such a course.

Yet that is just the way some people do live. They have a memory like a sieve, letting fall all the bright and joyous memories but retaining all the sad and bitter ones. They forget their pleasant experiences, their happy hours, and their days of

The Duty of Forgetting Sorrow

gladness; but they remember every painful event in their past lives. They will talk for hours of their past bereavements and griefs dwelling with a strange, morbid pleasure on each sad incident. They keep the old wounds in their hearts from healing by continually brooding over the reminiscences of their lost joys. They forget all their ten thousand blessings and joys in the absorbing recollections of the two or three sorrows they have experienced.

Tennyson makes Rizpah say, "The night has crept into my heart, and begun to darken my eyes." So it is with these people who live perpetually in the shadows and gloom of their sorrows. The darkness has crept into their souls, and all the brightness has passed out of their lives. Their visions have become so blurred that they can no longer discern the lovely colors in God's universe.

Few perversions of life are sadder than this fascination with the gloom and shadows of past griefs. It is the will of God that we should turn our eyes away from our sorrows and go on to the new duties and joys that await us. We cannot get back those we have lost by standing and

"WHOM THE LORD LOVETH"

weeping over their graves. When King David's child was dead, he dried his tears and went at once to God's house and worshiped, saying, **"Now he is dead, wherefore should I fast? can I bring him back again? I shall go to him, but he shall not return to me" (2 Samuel 12:23).** Instead of weeping over a grave, he turned his eyes toward heaven, where his child was waiting for him, and began with new ardor to press toward that home. He turned the pressure of his grief into the channels of holy living.

That is the way every believer in Christ should deal with his sorrows. Weeping inconsolably beside a grave can never bring back a loved one, nor can any blessing come out of such sadness. It does not make our hearts any softer or more Christlike; it only embitters us and stunts our spiritual growth.

There was a mother who lost her lovely daughter by death. For a long time the mother had been a consistent Christian, but when her child died she refused any comfort. Her pastor and other Christian friends sought to help draw her thoughts away from her grief, but all their efforts

The Duty of Forgetting Sorrow

were in vain. She would not look at anything but her sorrow. She spent a portion of nearly every day beside her daughter's grave. She refused to listen to any words of consolation, and she would not lift her eyes toward heaven, where her child had gone. She stopped going to church, where she had once loved to worship. She deliberately shut out of her heart every conception of God's love and kindness and thought of Him only as the powerful Being who had taken her child away from her. Because of the darkness of her inconsolable grief, the joy of her faith failed her. Her heart grew cold and sick with despair. She refused to submit to her loss and go on to the new joys that God wanted to give her.

There was another mother who also lost a child—one of the sweetest children God ever sent to this earth. The loss almost crushed the heart of this bereft mother, yet she did not sit down in the gloom and dwell there as had the other. She did not shut out the sunshine and thrust away the blessing of divine comfort. She recognized her Father's hand in her grief and bowed in submission to God's will. She opened her heart to the glorious truth of eternal life and was comforted by the simple faith that her child was with Christ. She remembered too that she had duties to the living, and she turned away from the grave where her little one slept to minister to those who still lived and needed her care and love. As a result, her life grew richer and more beautiful beneath its grief. She came from the deep shadow a lovelier Christian, and her home and the whole community shared the blessing that she had found in her sorrow.

It is easy to see which of these two ways of enduring sorrow is the right one. It is proper to tenderly cherish the memory of our Christian dead, but we should train ourselves to think of them as being in heaven with Christ waiting for us, not in the grave. When we submit to God and His plan for us, He will fill us with tranquillity even as we move over the waves of trial.

> He taketh that we may forever keep:
> All that makes life most beautiful and deep,
>   Our dearest hopes, by sorrow glorified,
>   Beneath His everlasting wings abide;
> For, oh, it is our true need to find
> Earth's vanished bliss in heavenly glory shrined.

The Duty of Forgetting Sorrow

The blessings that have gone away are not the only ones that God has for us. This summer's flowers will all fade by and by, but spring will come again, and beauty will cover the earth again. So the joys that have gone from our homes and hearts are not the only joys available to us. God has others to give us just as rich as those we have lost.

One of the most serious dangers of inconsolable sorrow is that our mourning for the dead may lead us to neglect our duty to the living. This we should never do. God does not desire us to give up our work because of a broken heart. We may not sit down beside the graves of our dead and linger there, cherishing our grief. **"Follow me; and let the dead bury their dead,"** the Master said to one who wished to bury his father and then follow Him (Matthew 8:22). The lesson is for all, and for all time. There is much to do. We will have scarcely laid our dead away before the earnest call of duty bids us hasten to new tasks.

The pressure is not always so intense, yet in all of our sorrows the principle is the same. God does not desire us to waste our life in tears. We are to put our grief into new energy for service. Sorrow should make us more reverent, more earnest, and more helpful to others. God's work must not suffer while we stop to weep. The work in the household, in the school, in the store, and in the field must go on again—the sooner the better.

Sometimes the death of one person is a divine voice calling another to a new duty. If a father dies, the mother has to shoulder a double responsibility. If he has a son that is old enough, it will be his duty to take up his father's work of supporting his family. When our loved ones pass away, our bereavement is a call to new duty, not to sad weeping.

It bids us do the work that they laid down;
  Take up the song where they broke off the strain;
So journey till we reach the heavenly town,
  Where are laid up our treasures and our crown,
And our lost loved ones will be found again.

Sometimes our work is less, not more, when death comes, as when a mother puts her baby or handicapped child into the grave. This is no excuse to be idle. Could it not be that God has taken from her hands the care and duty that had filled them, because He has some other work for them to do? He has set them free so that with their trained skill and their enriched sympathies they may serve others.

In a sickroom there was a little rosebush in a pot in a window. There was only one rose on the bush, and its face turned full toward the outside light. Someone came into the room and turned the pot so that the rose faced the room, but in a little time it resumed its old position. With wonderful persistence it refused to face the darkness of the room and insisted on looking toward the sunlight.

The flower has a lesson for us. We should never allow life's gloom and sorrows to distract us. Like the rose, we should turn our face away toward the light and receive strength for duty and service. Grief should always make us better Christians and give us new power. It should make our heart softer, our spirit kinder, and our touch more gentle. We should learn its lessons and then go on to new love and better service.

It is in this way that lonely hearts find their sweetest, richest comfort. When we

"WHOM THE LORD LOVETH"

sit and brood over our sorrows, the darkness deepens about us and our strength changes to weakness. But if we turn away from our gloom and take up the tasks of comforting and helping others, we shall grow stronger.

> When all our hopes are gone,
>   'Tis well our hands must still keep toiling on
>   For others' sake;
> For strength to bear is found in duty done,
>   And he is blest indeed who learns to make
>   The joy of others cure his own heartache.

CHAPTER TWELVE

Effectual Prayer

> We kneel how weak, we rise how full of power.
>   Why therefore should we do ourselves this
>   wrong,
> Or others—that we are not always strong,
>   That we are ever overborne with care,
> That we should ever weak or heartless be,
>   Anxious or troubled, when with us is prayer,
> And joy and strength and courage are with Thee?

"WHOM THE LORD LOVETH"

Effectual prayer is prayer that avails. The Bible tells us that **"the effectual fervent prayer of a righteous man availeth much" (James 5:16).** The Greek word translated *availeth* in this verse means "to have strength or power." We could say, "The effectual, fervent prayer of a righteous man has much power" without doing violence to the Scriptural teaching of this verse. Prayer is powerful. It works.

Some people claim that the effect of prayer exists only in our mind. They reason like this: A person feels troubled and pleads with God for relief. Because he believes that God has heard his prayer, it has a psychological effect on him, easing his troubled mind. He feels better, not because of a change in circumstances, but because of the therapeutic value of his prayer. So you have answered your own prayer. God had nothing to do with it.

No doubt there are many times when an answer to prayer appears to be nothing more than this to an unbelieving onlooker. Here are three Bible examples of prayers that a skeptic would say were unanswered. King David prayed for his sick child that it might live, but it died. When David knew that his child was dead, he washed away his tears and went to God's house and worshiped. When he returned to his home, the members of his household were astonished by the way he bore himself. He was no longer weeping, and he asked for food to eat. His prayer was not answered literally, but it had brought comfort to his heart.

The apostle Paul earnestly asked God three times to take away his "thorn in the flesh." Again, his prayer was not answered literally. God did not remove his painful affliction, but we know that God heard his prayer, because of the answer He gave: **"My grace is sufficient for thee: for my strength is made perfect in weakness."**

Paul accepted this answer gladly, without question or rebellion. He said, **"Most gladly therefore will I rather glory in my infirmities, that the power of Christ may rest upon me" (2 Corinthians 12:9).**

"WHOM THE LORD LOVETH"

Some people would say that his prayer was not answered, because he was not healed. But in another real sense it was, since his affliction no longer troubled him. He even rejoiced that he still had it, since it brought glory to God.

Is it a greater miracle to heal a person of his affliction, or to give him the strength to bear it for the rest of his life and be happy to do so? Anyone with any understanding of human character would agree that the second answer is the greatest miracle.

We have the third example in our Lord's experience in Gethsemane. He pleaded with God to remove the bitter cup of suffering from Him, but His request was not granted. Yet the anguish of His heart grew less and less intense until He was able to say, **"The cup which my Father hath given me, shall I not drink it?" (John 18:11).** His prayer did not deliver Him from the bitter experience into which He was entering, but it gave Him the strength to endure it without murmuring.

In all three of these cases God answered *no* to a sincere request from one of His own. Does this mean that God did not answer these prayers? Of course not! *No* is just as valid an answer as *yes*, when it comes from God. He gave an even greater miracle to each of the three; He gave them strength to bear their trial in victory.

If you have a friend who is carrying a heavy load, there are two ways to help him. You may take part of his burden and carry it for him, or you may encourage him, giving him the strength and vitality to carry it himself. The last way of helping is just as effective as the first, and often it is a great deal wiser.

We have a very poor understanding of prayer if we think that God will come running at every cry of ours, remove every burden we think is too heavy, or grant us every desire we might have. Often it would be an unkindness, and not love for God to grant what we ask of Him. Instead, He gives us strength to endure the trial and to rejoice in His will.

> Father, I do not ask
> That Thou wilt choose some other task
>   And make it mine. I pray
>   But this: Let every day
> Be molded still
> By Thine own hand; my will

"WHOM THE LORD LOVETH"

> Be only Thine, however deep
> I have to bend Thy hand to keep.
> Let me not simply do, but be content,
> Sure that the little crosses each are sent
> And no mistake can ever be
> With Thine own hand to choose for me.

God does answer *yes* to prayers, as well as *no*, when it is His will. When Elijah prayed fervently that it might not rain, there was no rain for three years and six months. Then he prayed again, and it rained. The Bible has many such illustrations. Every devout Christian could give some examples of answered prayer in his life. All true prayer is effectual. God hears every sincere prayer that a Christian prays, and He answers it in some way.

The Bible does mention several kinds of prayer that God will ignore. In the eighteenth chapter of Luke, the Pharisee did not receive a response to his prayer because of the pride of his heart. He had many things to tell God, but God ignored his prayer. The only prayer acceptable to God that the Pharisee could have prayed was the prayer of the publican whom he despised, who prayed, **"God be merciful**

Effectual Prayer

to me a sinner" (Luke 18:13).

The Book of James also mentions selfish prayers: **"Ye ask, and receive not, because ye ask amiss, that ye may consume it upon your lusts"** *(James 4:3).*

What, then, is effectual prayer? When the disciples asked Jesus to teach them to pray, He taught them the prayer we call the Lord's Prayer from which we can learn a number of lessons about effectual prayer.

To begin with, we must approach God, saying, "Our Father." This means that we must come to God in prayer as His children. One writes:

> My little girl tonight with childish glee,
>   Although her months had numbered not
>   two score,
>   Escaped her nurse, and at my study door,
> With tiny fingers rapping, spoke to me.
>   Though faint her words, I heard them tremblingly
> Fall from her lips as if the darkness bore
>   Its weight upon her: "Father's child!" No
>   more
> I waited for, but straightway willingly
>   Brought the sweet intruder into light
>   With happy laughter.

"WHOM THE LORD LOVETH"

This is the way that we should always come to God in prayer. Whenever we do, we need not doubt that the door will open to us.

We can learn much from the order of the petitions of the Lord's Prayer. When we come to God, we are prone to think first of our worries and desires. But that is not how the Master taught in His model prayer. We must first recognize the greatness and holiness of God, before we are ready to ask anything of Him.

Half of the Lord's Prayer is finished before there is a word about the earthly needs of him who is praying. We are to pray first for the hallowing of our Father's Name. It is a great deal more important that we in our own life shall be interpreters of God, than that our burdens shall be lifted away, our businesses prospered, our sorrows comforted. This will help us to see ourselves properly and keep us from the trap the Pharisee fell into in his prayer.

Next we are to pray for the coming of our Father's kingdom. How often do we pray that the return of the Lord would be soon? Do we have a burning desire to leave this world behind to be with Him in

Effectual Prayer

His kingdom? Or have the things of earth stolen our hearts?

Then we are to ask that God's will would be done in earth as it is in heaven. This requires laying down our will and accepting His, allowing the law of heaven to rule within our hearts. Do we really desire His will, or is prayer just a lever we use to try to get God to do our will?

It is not an accident that the Lord's Prayer is arranged as it is. The order teaches us priorities in prayer. We are not ready to approach God with our own personal desires until we recognize His holiness, long for His kingdom, and desire His will to be done in our lives.

> It is not prayer—
>   This clamor of our eager wants
> That fills the air
>   With wearying, selfish plaints.
>
> It is true prayer
>   To seek the Giver more than gift;
> God's life to share,
>   And love—for this our cry to lift.

It is comforting that it is not wrong to

ask God to supply our daily needs. He loves His children, and we should not be afraid to ask for the things we need, as long as we do not ask selfishly. Only we should never forget to keep our personal wants and troubles secondary to our longing for the things of God. We must put the honor and the interests of God and His cause above all else in our lives. Only then will our prayers be effectual.

Another condition of effectual prayer suggested in the Lord's Prayer is the spirit of forgiveness. Jesus regarded this as so important that He returned to it after His prayer to teach us, saying, **"For if ye forgive men their trespasses, your heavenly Father will also forgive you: but if ye forgive not men their trespasses, neither will your Father forgive your trespasses" (Matthew 6:14, 15).** It is very clear that forgiveness is an essential attitude in the heart of the man whose prayer God will hear and answer. Prayers born in a bitter, resentful heart do not find their way to heaven.

Indeed, the entire Lord's Prayer is a strong protest against selfishness. We come to God as our Father, not my Father.

We ask for our daily bread, not just enough for myself. When we plead for the forgiveness of our sins we ask forgiveness for others as well. Selfishness at the throne of grace makes the most eloquent pleading worthless. Love is a condition of effectual prayer.

There are other elements in an effectual prayer. Our Lord teaches us that we must be persistent. **"Men ought always to pray, and not to faint" (Luke 18:1).** Maybe God has not answered our prayers because we lack earnestness.

Faith is another essential. Prayer without faith has no power. Jesus said in Matthew 17:20 that if a person has faith as a grain of mustard seed, he will be able to remove mountains. In other words, he will be able to overcome the greatest difficulties and obstacles. When we pray in faith, we enter into a close fellowship with Jesus. Such believing attaches us to Him so that His life flows through us. Nothing is impossible to the person who believes.

The lowliest and feeblest of God's children have the privilege of prevailing in prayer, laying hold upon God's strength. We may make intercession for others and

"WHOM THE LORD LOVETH"

be assured that God heard our prayers. All the power of heaven is within the reach of him who prays.

> Whate'er is good to wish, ask that of Heaven,
>   Though it be what thou canst not hope to see;
> Pray to be perfect, though material leaven
>   Forbid the spirit so on earth to be;
> But if for any wish thou dar'st not pray,
>   Then pray to God to cast that wish away.

CHAPTER THIRTEEN

The Humbling of Self

We mar our work for God by noise and bustle;
Can we not do our part and not be heard?
Why should we care
That men should see us with our tools
And praise the skill with which we use them?

"WHOM THE LORD LOVETH"

Humility is one of the most difficult lessons for all of us to learn. It is the effacement of self. Self always dies hard. It seems to us that we have a right to put our name on every piece of work we do and to get full honor for it. We like to have people know of our self-sacrifices and appreciate the good things we do.

Yet we all know that our Lord does not approve of such an attitude toward ourselves and our work. In Matthew 6:1 Jesus expressly commands His followers not to do their alms before men, to be seen of them.

We must often do our good deeds before men; indeed, Jesus commands us, **"Let your light so shine before men, that they may see your good works, and glorify your Father" (Matthew 5:16).** It is not the doing of good deeds before men but doing them to be seen of men that is condemned. We

The Humbling of Self

are not to live for human praise but for God's approval.

There were those who made a show of their prayers by praying on street corners and other conspicuous places so that men would see them, and honor them for their piety. Such people get what they seek—men do see them. But God does not hear them. Jesus told His disciples that they should enter into their closet and shut the door when they prayed. Public prayer has its place. Indeed, Jesus prayed in public, but our acts of devotion should be for the eye of God alone. We should never do anything to get human notice and commendation.

We should apply this teaching to everything in our lives. Everything we do we should do to please God. Jesus said of Himself, **"I do always those things that please him" (John 8:29).** He did His works for divine approval, not for the praise of men. It did not matter to Him whether anyone but God knew what He was doing.

If we can learn this lesson of living and working for God's approval only, it will set us free of the bondage of desiring the praise of men. It will give us a wonderful sense of freedom, will exalt our ideals of life and duty, and will inspire us always to our best.

John the Baptist illustrated the grace of humility—self-effacement—in his life and ministry. When he first began to preach, great throngs of people flocked after him. But when Jesus began to preach, the crowds melted away from John and went after the new prophet. Instead of being envious of Jesus, John rejoiced in seeing Him honored, though at the cost of his own fame. When his disciples complained to him about Jesus, John answered, **"He must increase, but I must decrease" (John 3:30).** He understood that the highest and noblest use of his life was to add to the honor of his Master. He was glad to be unnoticed so that the glory of Christ might shine brighter.

Such self-denial should characterize every Christian. We should seek to get recognition for Jesus and be willing to be unrecognized and unhonored ourselves. It is a mark of spiritual attainment to be willing to be anonymous in every service for Christ. While it is not always possible to remain unidentified when we do a good

The Humbling of Self

deed, we should always do it with a desire to please and honor Christ, not ourselves.

We should seek to put aside altogether every thought of what is to come to us from the things we do. The faintest trace of a desire for reward in our spirit in any service we may be rendering to another leaves a blot upon the deed and spoils its beauty. The true reward of kindness or self-denial is that which comes from the act itself, the joy of helping another, of relieving distress, of making the heart a little braver and stronger for the toil or struggle that we cannot make easier.

Are we willing to keep quiet about the good deeds we have done? The Lord condemned those who sounded a trumpet before them when they were giving alms. When we talk about our piety or about our good deeds and acts of self-denial and helpfulness, we are guilty of the same sin they were.

Henry Drummond wrote: "Put a seal upon your lips and forget what you have done. After you have [done good] . . . go back into the shade again and say nothing about it."

We should not even spend time thinking

about the good deeds we have done. Instead, we should simply consider them having been our duty to do, and leave them behind us. Pride will always spoil the beauty of a good deed, no matter how well done.

Let your good deeds be forgotten on earth, even by yourself. There is a place where they will all be written down. That is record enough.

CHAPTER FOURTEEN

Godly Character Refinement

To nobly think the highest thought that I can reach,
  To feel the mighty thrill of kindling
    aspiration,
To hate with ardent soul all base, ignoble schemes,
  To match a steadfast will against the
    tempter's arts,
To do my daily duty in heroic mood,
  To take my cross and follow Christ
    unmurmuringly,
To love my fellow men as truly as myself,
  To feed the hungry mouth, to clothe the
    naked back,
To visit them that sit in dismal prison cells,
  To love my God with all my heart and
    soul and strength—
Such holy work as this is heaven begun on earth.

"WHOM THE LORD LOVETH"

Every Christian will find some weak spots in his character and some rough edges to smooth over as he continues in his Christian life. Some people lack the qualities of gentleness and thoughtfulness that belong to the true Christian character. They are sometimes rude, trampling under their feet those who are more frail than themselves.

Others lack self-control. They have not learned that **"he that is slow to anger is better than the mighty; and he that ruleth his spirit than he that taketh a city" (Proverbs 16:32).** Few faults mar the beauty and the influence of a life more than the habit of ill temper. One person writes: "Losing the temper takes all the sweet, pure feeling out of life. You may get up in the morning with a clean heart, full of song, and start out as happy as a bird; and the moment you are crossed and you give way to your temper, the clean feeling vanishes and a load as heavy as lead is rolled upon your heart, and you go through the rest of the day feeling like a culprit, unless you promptly repent of the sin you have committed, confess your fault, and seek forgiveness of God and man."

Some lack love. Love must always be the ruling element in Christian character. Fine manners may be the result of the study of the rules of etiquette, but no manners are beautiful that are not the fruit of love in the heart. Gentleness belongs to Christian character, and gentleness is love in action.

It is every Christian's duty to daily grow more like his Master. It is important for us to take heed if God shows us deficiencies in our lives such as the ones mentioned earlier. No Christian wants his character to have ungodly blemishes, because they are a reproach to his Master and will separate him from his God if he allows them to remain in his life.

Many books are written that attempt to help people improve their characters. However, most of them teach self-control and self-discipline using humanistic methods that have their origin in worldly systems of self-improvement. All of these fail miserably in their goal of helping people to become better Christians, because they depend on the power of the flesh to bring it about.

There is only one power that can make us more like Christ. If we allow the Holy Spirit to take control of our lives, He will make of us what God wants and will provide all the character-refining influences that we need to become more Christlike. We can never achieve in ourselves the spiritual beauty we yearn for, nor by any mere self-discipline attain the gentleness, the peace, and the graces that belong to the true spiritual character. But God is ready to work in us and with us if we will admit Him into our lives, and then our striving to grow into loveliness will not be in vain.

A personal friendship with Christ has a deep influence on our characters. If we live with Him in close, daily companionship, walking with Him, talking with Him, and dwelling in the atmosphere of His presence continually, our rough edges will be transformed into spiritual refinement and our earthliness into heavenliness.

A friend bought a common clay jar for a few cents and filled it with some rare perfume. After a time the jar became so saturated with the rich fragrance that it had a beautiful aroma even after it was completely empty. So it is with our lives when Christ fills them. The sweetness of His love and the holiness of His Spirit permeate us until our dispositions, thoughts, feelings, and affections become like Christ and our lives are the partakers and the expressions of His divine nature.

One important area of our lives where this Christlikeness will become very evident is in our manners. Some people think that it makes small difference what kind of manners a person has, as long as he is genuine in character. But this is not true. A man may have the best of intentions, but if he is rude and awkward, lacking refinement, much of the value of his goodness is lost.

Manners are very important. In business, courtesy is almost as important as capital. A man who is discourteous may have fine goods in his store, but people will not come to buy of him. On the other hand, an agreeable man who treats his customers politely, is patient, kind, and thoughtful, and is always ready to oblige and desirous to please will attract patrons to his place and build up a business. No merchant will retain in his employ a salesperson who treats customers rudely.

The same is true in all occupations. The surly, discourteous doctor will not get patients. If you begin to deal with a tradesman who appears to be impertinent, cross-tempered, and disobliging, you will not continue to go to him.

The principal of a private school was very popular with his boys and for some years did splendid work. During this time the school prospered. Then something happened that soured the principal and embittered his spirit. He became stern, severe, and harsh. He would give way to fits of violent temper and used language in the presence of his pupils that no gentleman should ever use. One year of this was enough to break up the school.

We all know the impressions that the manners of people make upon us when we first meet them. Well-mannered behavior goes a long way in winning our favor and confidence, while poor manners tend to turn us against a person.

When a Christian has rude manners, he not only turns people against himself but also against Christ. It does not please God when His people have poor manners. The Bible states that He suffered, or endured, the manners of the children of Israel for forty years in the wilderness, implying His displeasure. There is no doubt that the manners of the children of Israel were very bad. They were always murmuring and complaining. They did not praise God for His care but were constantly ungrateful and rebellious. It shows the marvelous patience of God that He put up with their manners all those years.

This habit of fretting and complaining about one's condition or circumstances is still far too common among some professing Christians. There are some people who seem to find their greatest pleasure in talking about their discomforts and miseries, their ill health, and their trials. They do not seem to realize how discourteous they are, both to those who must listen to them, and to God, who has

"WHOM THE LORD LOVETH"

blessed them abundantly in many ways. "By the grace of God I never fret," said Wesley. "I am discontented with nothing. And to have persons at my ear fretting and murmuring at everything is like tearing the flesh off my bones."

An old writer says,

> Fret not: 'tis wasteful,
>   For it spoils thy work;
> And selfish, for
>   It doth thy neighbor irk;
> And faithless:
>   Did not God thy lot prepare?
> But chiefly needless,
>   Being healed by prayer.

The Bible is the best book of manners ever written. It says:

"And though I bestow all my goods to feed the poor, and though I give my body to be burned, and have not charity, it profiteth me nothing. Charity suffereth long, and is kind; charity envieth not; charity vaunteth not itself, is not puffed up, doth not behave itself unseemly, seeketh not

her own, is not easily provoked, thinketh no evil; rejoiceth not in iniquity, but rejoiceth in the truth; beareth all things, believeth all things, hopeth all things, endureth all things."
1 Corinthians 13:3–7

The Christian who practices this will be well-mannered.

Many times people are rude without intending to be, because they do not stop to think before they talk or act. When a man learns that some word or act of his has hurt someone, he may try to excuse himself by saying, "I did not know they were so sensitive about that." If he had been more thoughtful, he would have known, and he would not have spoken the word or done the thing that hurt another. To be rude because of carelessness is almost as serious as being rude on purpose.

To have Christian manners we need to bring every expression of our lives under the control of the love of Christ. It is easy enough to be gentle to men who are gentle to us. But it is harder to be gentle to people who are continually doing or saying things that irritate us.

But our manners should be unaffected by the characters and reactions of others. Jesus was not rude to those who were rude to Him. He loved those who treated him unjustly just as much as those who were kind to Him. He was as gracious to the discourteous and the unkind as He was to those who were courteous to Him. If we have the mind that was in Christ Jesus, we too will be unaffected by the atmosphere about us. Love beareth all things and endureth all things.

The best school of manners is the school of Christ. We are not ready to relate to our fellow man in a Christlike fashion until we have allowed Him to mold our character and our manners through the work of the Holy Spirit in us.

CHAPTER FIFTEEN

The Secret of Serving

Rouse to some work of high and holy love,
    And thou an angel's happiness shalt know,
Shalt bless the earth; while in the world above,
    The good begun by thee shall onward flow
In many a branching stream, and wider grow.
    The seed that in these few and fleeting hours
Thy hands unsparing and unwearied sow
    Shall deck thy grave with amaranthine flowers
And yield thee fruits divine
    In heaven's imperial bowers.

"WHOM THE LORD LOVETH"

Before we can help people, we must love them. This is the weakness of most secular welfare schemes. They are only systems without a heart of love to inspire them. A paid agent may dispense charity very justly and generously, but his gifts only feed the body. There are deeper needs than those of the body. When love brings the gift of bread, it feeds two hungers—the hunger of the body and the hunger of the heart.

But the practice of charity is not the only place where love is necessary. Love is the true secret of power in all areas of life. It is the essential qualification for being a pastor, a teacher, or a personal worker. Without love we are not qualified to do God's work.

First we must have a fervent love for Christ. A person who does not love Jesus more than anything or anyone else is not truly His disciple and certainly is not fitted to care for Christ's sheep and lambs. But if we truly love Christ, we will also love our brethren. No one can do Christ's work who does not love his fellow men.

We must have love to help others. It is not enough for the preacher to declare to all men that God loves them. The preacher must love them too if he wants them to believe his message. The true evangelist shows others the love of God working in a human life. If we would win men for God, we must show the tenderness of God by our tenderness. We must reveal the compassion of God by our compassion. We give ourselves to others in His service because He gave us the gift of salvation.

A man is not ready to preach the cross until he has taken up the cross himself. He must love men enough to give himself for them, or his preaching will not have any power. It was this that gave Jesus such influence over men and drew the people to Him in such throngs. He told them of the love of God, but they also saw that love portrayed in His own life. He performed many miracles. But it was the love in His heart that made His ministry so meaningful.

Only love can meet the real needs of men. Power has its ways of helping. Law may protect. Money will buy bread and build houses. But only love enables us to give men what they need most—the gift of compassion. Many a person has found Christ and had his deepest spiritual needs met because a Christian gave him the compassion that his inner being craved, proving to him that God loved him too.

True love fills our hearts with the desire to serve others as Christ did. It is difficult for ungodly people to understand the Christian's desire to serve others. The world's attitude is that of selfishness and self-interest. Men want to be served by others, not to give service to others. They associate with other men, hoping to have their own personal interests advanced through their relationship. Even their friendships often have the selfish motive of gaining something in return.

But the love of Christ teaches us to look at others in an altogether different way. Instead of asking how they can help us, it teaches us to ask how we may help them.

The Secret of Serving

Jesus said of Himself, **"The Son of man came not to be ministered unto, but to minister" (Mark 10:45).** A study of His life proves this statement. He used all His authority and power in serving others and doing them good. The picture of Jesus with a basin and a towel is a true representation of His whole life. He lived to serve.

Jesus needed to teach His disciples this lesson. They seemed to feel that their friendship with Jesus would get them special favors from God. Two of them even asked for the special privilege of sitting beside Him in heaven. They needed to learn what true greatness really is. Jesus told them,

> **"Ye know that they which are accounted to rule over the Gentiles exercise lordship over them; and their great ones exercise authority upon them. But so shall it not be among you: but whosoever will be great among you, shall be your minister: and whosoever of you will be the chiefest, shall be servant of all."**
> **Mark 10:42–44**

"WHOM THE LORD LOVETH"

The noblest life is the one that serves others.

This does not mean that a servant is always greater than his master, or his work more pleasing to God. The master may be serving others too. It is not our position but our spirit that determines our rank.

The law of love requires us to look upon everyone with a desire for his good and with a readiness to help him. We are a debtor to every man, owing to each a debt of love and service. If the love of Christ is in us, it will inspire us with kind thoughts of everyone. We will not think so much of having friends as of being a friend; of receiving, as of giving; of being helped, as of helping. On the other hand, we will not force our service on anyone who does not want our help. We will not help simply for the sake of helping, or look down on those we have helped as being inferior to us. It is Christlike to love, and loving will make us more Christlike.

This spirit of service prepares us to be truly helpful to others. Then we will look upon everyone we meet as our brother. Even the most debased will appear to us

The Secret of Serving

as still having in him possibilities of something noble and beautiful.

When we see every person we meet as a possible future Christian, whatever his present character or worth, we shall find ample inspiration for service. It was this that drew Jesus to His wondrous ministry among the lost: He saw what it was possible for them to become. We are debtors to everyone, and if we are truly following our Master, we will love everyone and be ready to serve them in love.

An interesting story is told of a good woman who opened a home for unwanted children. Among those she received into her home was a forlorn little boy of three years old. He had blotchy skin, and his disposition was fretful and unhappy. Try as she would, the woman could not love him. Something about his person repelled her. She was outwardly kind to him, but it was always an effort to show him any tenderness.

One day she sat on the verandah of her house with this boy on her knee. She dropped asleep and dreamed that she saw the Master bending over her. She heard Him say, "If I can bear with you, who are so full of fault and sin, can you not, for My sake, love this poor, innocent child, who is suffering, not for his own sin, but because of the sin of his parents?"

The woman awoke with a sudden start and looked into the face of the boy. Penitent because of her past unkind feeling, and with a new compassion for him in her heart, she bent down and kissed him as tenderly as ever she kissed her own child. The boy gave her a smile so sweet that she had never seen one like it before. From that moment a change came over him. The new affection in the woman's heart transformed his peevish, fretful disposition into gentleness. She loved him now, and her serving was glad-hearted and Christlike, and no longer perfunctory.

This is the secret of serving. We must love those we would help. Service without love counts for nothing. We can love even the unloveliest when we learn to see in them the possibilities of divine beauty. But only the love of Christ in us will prepare us for such service.

CHAPTER SIXTEEN

Thinking Soberly

One small life in God's great plan—
    How futile it seems as the ages roll,
Do what it may or strive how it can
    To alter the sweep of the infinite whole!
A single stitch in an endless web,
A drop in the ocean's flow and ebb!
    But the pattern is rent where the stitch is lost,
    Or marred where the tangled threads have crossed;
And each life that fails of its true intent
Mars the perfect plan that the Master meant.
                  —*Susan Coolidge*

"WHOM THE LORD LOVETH"

Even the most insignificant life has an enormous influence on those around it. Therefore we should never feel that our lives are unimportant or useless. Yet we should also remain humble, for in God's sight even the greatest are very small. It is good to be realistic about ourselves in the world because it is easy to have an exalted opinion of oneself. Self-conceit will quickly exaggerate our importance and our influence among men. However, we may also have too low an opinion of our worth as a redeemed child of God and of our abilities, causing us to shrink from our duties and to refuse to meet life's responsibilities.

In Romans 12:3, the apostle Paul encourages each follower of Christ **"not to think of himself more highly than he ought to think; but to think soberly, according as God hath dealt to every man**

Thinking Soberly

the measure of faith." He then uses the human body to illustrate further what he is talking about. A human body has many different parts, each of which has different functions. Similarly, not all Christians have the same gifts or are fitted by God to perform the same duty. Some have the gift of prophesying, others of ministering, others of exhortation, and so forth.

This verse also tells us to think soberly. Thinking soberly includes recognizing that God has given our gifts to us. This takes away all ground for glorying in our abilities as though they were of our own making.

Even if our abilities are greater than our neighbor's, we have no right to boast or become proud because of it. By whose standard are they greater? God has given him the abilities he needs to perform his duties. God has given us different duties to fulfill than our neighbor, so He has given us the abilities we need to perform them. If we recognize this truth, we will not be proud; instead, we will humbly give God the praise and honor for giving us the gifts we need to do His will.

It is impossible to think soberly if we

leave God out of our thoughts. An artist was watching a student paint a landscape bathed in the glory of the setting sun. In the foreground stood a large barn. The artist watched the young man quietly for a while, and then said to him, "If you spend so much time painting the shingles on the barn, you will never have time to paint the sunset. You will have to choose between the two."

There are many people who put shingles before sunsets in their lives. They see the dusty road on which they are walking, but not the glorious sky that arches above them. They toil for earth's perishing things and miss heaven's imperishable glory that might have been theirs. They spend all their lives in striving to get honor, wealth, or power, and they miss God. They paint the shingles into their picture, bringing out every minutest detail, only to discover that the glory of the sunset has vanished and they have but a picture of some shingles. Thinking soberly is putting God and eternal things first in our lives. If we fail in this, nothing else that we may do will be of any avail. Without God, our life is valueless.

Thinking Soberly

Sober thinking will give us a proper viewpoint of our abilities. Since every ability God gives is for a need, we should not evaluate abilities as being important or unimportant, or classify them as being humble or being great. One man may be an eloquent speaker and be able to move and thrill hearts. Another is a quiet man, with little to say in public, but he has the gift of intercession. While the first man preaches, this man prays. Should the preacher glory over his brother who cannot speak so impressively but who has learned the power of prayer instead? The second man's prayers may be as powerful in moving the hearts of men to repentance as the first man's eloquence.

Often the abilities that win the praise and regard of men are not the abilities that reach the highest into heaven or the deepest into men's hearts. It may be that the great preacher's words would have no power over men to bring them to God but for the lowly brother who sits in the congregation and prays.

The man who thinks soberly does not forget that great gifts are great only according to the manner in which they are used. The abilities that God gives us are not for the adornment of our lives; they are given to us for His service. God never gives abilities to make one person greater than another. The humblest member of the body who faithfully fulfills his function is honorable. But this gives him no reason to think highly of himself or to belittle other members and their functions. The lowliest Christian who does well the humblest work God gives him, using his abilities faithfully in service to men and for the honor of God, is realizing God's plan for his life. He is pleasing God just as well as the person who possesses a spectacular ability to do a work that seems greater in the eyes of men.

Instead of glorying in the attractiveness of his gift or power, each man should accept it as a responsibility committed to him by God. Each Christian should consecrate his own particular ability to God and then use it.

"Having then gifts differing according to the grace that is given to us, whether prophecy, let us prophesy according to the proportion of faith;

Thinking Soberly

> *or ministry, let us wait on our ministering: or he that teacheth, on teaching; or he that exhorteth, on exhortation: he that giveth, let him do it with simplicity."*
> **Romans 12:6–8**

This is the way thinking soberly about our lives should inspire us to use our gift. Instead of boasting of our abilities and thinking of ourselves more highly than we ought to think, we should use our particular ability to its very utmost to bring glory to God. Many a person with few natural gifts makes his life radiant by its service of love, while the man who has brilliant talents but does nothing with his gifts for God's glory allows his gifts to die, unused in his brain and heart.

There are many reasons not to think of ourselves more highly than we ought to think but to think soberly. Our abilities should give us a sense of responsibility instead of making us vain and self-conceited. We are to use our abilities, whether great or small, to bring glory to God. Someday we will have to give an account to God for them, both for their development and for their use. If we understand this, we will think soberly and humbly about our lives.

> "As every man hath received the gift, even so minister the same one to another, as good stewards of the manifold grace of God."
> 1 Peter 4:10

CHAPTER SEVENTEEN

Facing Disagreeable Situations

> There is no noble height thou canst not climb;
> All triumphs may be thine in time's futurity,
> If whatsoe'er thy fault, thou dost not faint or halt,
> But lean upon the staff of God's security.
> Earth has no claim the soul cannot contest.
> Know thyself part of the supernal source,
> And naught can stand before thy spirit's force;
> The soul's divine inheritance is best.

"WHOM THE LORD LOVETH"

Many people fail in life because they lack courage to endure disagreeable circumstances. They look for a career with only pleasant experiences. They want good results without the toil it costs other men to reach them. They wish to stand upon the mountain peaks, but they are unwilling to climb the steep, rugged paths that lead up to them. They desire success in life, but they are not ready to work for it. They dream beautiful dreams, but they do not have the skill or the energy to turn their dreams into realities.

They would like to leave the disagreeable out of every part of life. They are impatient with a disagreeable environment. They dislike disagreeable people and do not have the good nature and grace necessary to get along with them. They complain bitterly when they must

Facing Disagreeable Situations

suffer any inconvenience, when the weather is uncomfortable, when circumstances are unfavorable, or when they are sick. They cannot bear disappointment, and they chafe and fret when things do not turn out as they expected.

But there is nothing manly or noble in such an attitude toward life. It is impossible to find a path in this world where everything is totally agreeable. There always are thorns where there are roses, and usually they grow on the same stalk. There are some dark, unpleasant days in the brightest summer. There is usually at least one disagreeable person in every crowd. Even the pleasantest person will not be perfectly agreeable every hour of the 365 days in the year.

Not only are disagreeable circumstances inevitable in life, but they are also the school in which we learn our best lessons. Nothing noble and worthy is ever attained easily. The best things in life take hard work to accomplish.

Some people dream of genius as a gift that makes work unnecessary. They imagine that with this wondrous ability they can do the finest things without learning to do them. They fancy, for example, that genius can paint a beautiful picture without having touched brushes before; or write a story that will thrill hearts without ever having studied the mechanics of composition; or go into business and build up a great fortune without having had any business experience.

But such thoughts of life are only idle dreams. A genius is a person with "an infinite capacity for taking pains." Those who expect results without work will be bitterly disappointed in the end. Nothing beautiful or worthwhile was ever achieved without toil.

"Wherever a great thought is born, there also has been a Gethsemane." The best works of human creation have all cost a great price. Somebody's heart's blood has gone into every stanza of a sweet song and into every paragraph that inspires men. The Anglo-Saxon root of the word *bless* means "blood." We can bless another only by giving of our lifeblood. Doing good involves tears and suffering.

Not only are these painful processes necessary to produce results that are

Facing Disagreeable Situations

worthwhile, but they help our character to become beautiful and noble. Work is the only means of growth. Instead of being a curse, as some would have us believe, work is a means of doing good. The person who does not learn to work will always remain partly undeveloped. The things that we may achieve by working are not half so important as the things that work achieves in us.

> Disappointment is not utter failure;
> The striving is a measure of success.
> Each wise attempt but makes us stronger grow,
> Till, oft-repeated, stumbling blocks seem less
> And finally prove the steppingstones to gain
> The end in view, and our fond hopes attain!

A certain writer wrote an essay entitled: "Blessed Be Drudgery!" We owe the best things in our life and character to the things we ordinarily call drudgery. Children do not like getting up and leaving for school at the same hour every day. They tire of rules, bells, lessons, and tasks; but it is in this very drudgery of home and school that the child is being given the needed training for life. The child who misses such discipline, doing whatever he feels like doing, may be envied by his peers, but he is missing a tremendous blessing. "Blessed be drudgery!"

It is in the tiresome routine of hours, tasks, and rules that we learn the qualities that belong to true manhood. If we train our children from childhood to be prompt and systematic, they will carry their good habits into adult life, where these qualities will mean much to their success. If we can teach our children to pay their debts on the day, always keep every promise and appointment, and never be late, we will do them a great favor.

Annoying things play an important part in the making of life. We can try to shirk them if we will, but if we do we throw away a good opportunity because annoying things help us to grow. Young people should determine that they will never shrink from any task, toil, or self-discipline that faces them. Beyond these drudgeries of life are rewards that we cannot reach and possess in any other way.

It is a great loss to a young man to be born rich and not to have to ask, "What shall I do for a living?" unless he has in him the courage to enter life as if he was a poor man and to learn to work as if he had to. There is no other way to develop a manly character. There is no other way to make life worthwhile.

We are foolish and shortsighted indeed if we despise the disagreeable things God sends us. The disagreeable is inevitable. We will never find a perfect place or position in this world. Nor can we afford to miss the things that are less pleasant.

We shrink from life's hard battles, but it is through struggle and victory that we win the prizes of noble character. We dread sorrow, but it is through sorrow's bitterness that we find life's deepest, truest joy. We hold our life back from sacrifice, but it is only through losing our life that we can ever really save it. If we have faith and courage to *welcome* struggle, cost, pain, and sacrifice, we shall find our feet on the path to the best things in this world and the next.

> Then welcome each rebuff
> That turns earth's smoothness rough,
> Each sting that bids not sit nor stand,
> But go!

"WHOM THE LORD LOVETH"

Be our joys three parts pain!
Strive and hold cheap the strain;
Learn, nor account the pang; dare, never grudge
The throe!

CHAPTER EIGHTEEN

The Duty of Thanksgiving

Lord, in the sky of blue,
    No stain of cloud appears;
Gone all my faithless fears,
    Only Thy love seems true.

Help me to thank Thee, then, I pray,
Walk in the light and cheerfully obey!

"WHOM THE LORD LOVETH"

Every Christian should be a thankful person. Just think back for a moment to the time before you were a Christian. Can you remember the struggles you had? the guilt? the fear? the sleepless nights and the miserable days? Can you also remember the peace and joy that flooded your soul when you finally allowed God to have His way in your life? Are you still experiencing them? Then you have every reason to be thankful. There are many people in the world who are not enjoying what you are enjoying today, if you are a Christian. Have you thanked God today for saving your soul?

When you became a Christian, you gave up many things. You gave up an eternity in the fires of hell for the privilege of being forever in heaven. You gave up the bondage of sin for a life of victory over it. You traded the guilt in your life for the joy

The Duty of Thanksgiving

of knowing that your sins are forgiven. You do not have to lie awake at night anymore, fearing death or other calamities, because God is now in control of your future. Are you thankful for deliverance from what you gave up? and for what God has given you in return?

When you look at the long faces of some Christians, you almost have to wonder if they are grateful for what the Lord has done for them. They almost look as though they wish they could go back to what they had before God saved them. In fact, being unthankful is often one of the first steps that a person takes that leads him back to the old life of sin that he had left behind.

The Bible records various incidents of people who forgot what God had done for them and lost their salvation as a result. The apostle Paul was talking about such people when he said, **"Because that, when they knew God, they glorified him not as God, neither were thankful; but became vain in their imaginations, and their foolish heart was darkened" (Romans 1:21).** It is dangerous to be unthankful.

Notice all the reasons the psalmist

gives for being thankful in the following verses.

> "**O give thanks unto the Lord, for he is good: for his mercy endureth for ever. Let the redeemed of the Lord say so, whom he hath redeemed from the hand of the enemy. . . . Oh that men would praise the Lord for his goodness, and for his wonderful works to the children of men!"**
> **Psalm 107:1, 2, 8**

Christians who are grateful for what God has done for them will not only thank Him for what He has done for them but will tell other people about it too. The psalmist says, **"Let the redeemed of the Lord say so,"** and if we are truly grateful to Him for redeeming us, we will tell others what He has done for us.

Thankfulness is a Bible command. There are many verses besides the ones quoted here that tell us to be thankful. The Scriptures command us to praise oftener than they tell us to pray. Too many people come to God with requests, and then forget to thank Him after He has

The Duty of Thanksgiving

answered them. Ten lepers once cried to Jesus, begging Him to heal them. He heard them and graciously granted their plea. But only one of the ten returned to thank Him after He healed them.

Jesus keenly felt the ingratitude of the lepers who did not return. **"Where are the nine?"** He asked (Luke 17:17). God pours out His gifts and blessings upon His children every day. We disappoint Him when we are not thankful in return.

Every fall in our nation a day is set apart for giving thanks. However, if we are not thankful during the rest of the year, our ceremonies on Thanksgiving Day will not impress God either. Thanksgiving should be a daily experience for us, not a yearly one. It should be a way of life, something we would miss immediately if we were to lose it.

We need to train ourselves to be thankful. When we see a beautiful sunset or a rainbow, we should breathe a prayer of thanks for the beauty of creation and the ability to see. When we sit down to eat, we should thank God for our taste buds and for the food He has again provided. When we go to bed, we should thank Him for

"WHOM THE LORD LOVETH"

the ability to sleep and become rested for another day. When we awake, we should thank Him for His protection and for another day to serve Him, as well as for health and strength and the multitude of other blessings He gives us.

Sit down for a few hours and make a list of all the things you can think of for which you should be thankful. The list will be so long that it will drive you to your knees in gratitude and in repentance for your unthankfulness.

If we allow our hearts to cherish hatred, bitterness, evil thoughts, and hard feelings, we will not hear the music of love that breathes everywhere, pouring out from the heart of God. But if we keep our hearts gentle, patient, lowly, and kind, we will always hear the sweet strains of divine music from heaven, and we will find things to be thankful for everywhere we go.

A certain man used to say that the habit of cheerfulness was worth ten thousand dollars a year. This is not only true in a financial way. It will increase your enjoyment of life and your worth to others. It will even make you healthier. A glad

The Duty of Thanksgiving

heart gets much more out of life than a gloomy one does.

Every day brings its blessings. If it is raining, we can thank God for the rain. If trouble comes, God draws nearer than before, for **"as thy days, so shall thy strength be" (Deuteronomy 33:25).** If there is sorrow, we thank God for His comfort. If the day brings difficulties, hardships, heavy burdens, or sharp struggles, we remember that life's best things often come through just this kind of experience, and not in the easy ways. The thankful heart finds treasure and good everywhere.

A thankful person brings cheer wherever he goes. He leaves an unbroken trail of sunbeams behind him. Everybody is better as well as happier for meeting a person whose life is full of brightness and cheer.

> Just being happy
> >Is a fine thing to do;
>
> Looking on the bright side
> >Rather than the blue;
>
> Sad or sunny musing
> >Is largely in the choosing
>
> And just being happy
> >Is brave work and true.

"WHOM THE LORD LOVETH"

    Just being happy
        Helps other souls along;
    Their burdens may be heavy,
        And they may not be strong;
    And your own sky will lighten
        If other skies you brighten
    By just being happy
        With a heart full of song!

CHAPTER NINETEEN

"Charity Never Faileth"

> If I had the time to find a place
> And sit me down full face to face
>   With my better self, that cannot show
>   In my daily life that rushes so;
> It might be then I would see my soul
> Was stumbling still toward the shining goal;
>   I might be nerved by the thought sublime
>   If I had the time!
>
> —*Richard Burton*

"WHOM THE LORD LOVETH"

Jesus loved everyone, whether they were good or evil. He did not allow the character or the reactions of any person to decrease His love for others. Even when those He helped returned evil for His good, He did not stop loving and doing good. His fountain of love did not dry up from the bitterest hatred and persecutions of others. One man might prove to be unworthy of His compassion and unselfishness, by returning ingratitude and injury for the good He did for him, but the next one who came to Him with his needs did not find Him embittered by it. His love was as tender as if He had never received a hurt.

The Master commanded all His followers to be like Him in this. He instructed His disciples, "**This is my commandment, That ye love one another, as I have loved you**" **(John 15:12)**. We are to love our enemies as

Jesus loved His enemies. When others mistreat us, we are to pray for them instead of becoming bitter toward them in our hearts. We are to show to others the same forgiveness that we seek from God for ourselves.

It is our natural tendency to resent wrongs done to us and to allow the treatment we receive from others to affect our disposition. This is one point that we need to watch carefully in our lives. But if we would be like Jesus, we must not allow the reactions of others to chill the warmth of our love or check the flow of our kindness.

The old teaching was that one should forgive another three times. Peter thought he was taking a great stride forward when he suggested that a Christian should forgive seven times. But Jesus set the standard far beyond Peter's, saying, **"Not seven times, but seventy times seven" (Matthew 18:22).** In other words, our forgiveness is to be unending. No matter how often another person may repeat his offense against us, we are still to be ready to forgive. The same is true of patience, of compassion, of kindness, and of all goodness. The love in our hearts is to be unfailing, like a spring of water that never runs dry.

There are many things that discourage our kindness. Ingratitude is too common. Many times those we try to help prove unworthy, and nothing comes of our efforts to help them. They promise to do better but soon return to their old way of life. They take our favors and enjoy our gifts, and pay us with neglect or injustice. Too frequently those for whom we have done the most make the smallest return. It is easy to allow such experiences to discourage us and keep us from trying to help others, since nothing comes of it.

This is especially true of trying to help others by giving or lending them money. No other form of kindness proves unsatisfactory as often as this one does. Very seldom do gifts of money bring gratitude. For some reason the acceptance of such help seems to have a bad influence upon the feelings. Very few people remain close friends with those to whom they have given financial assistance.

For this reason it is usually best for us to give such gifts anonymously, perhaps through the deacon of our church or with the aid of a circumspect friend, rather than directly. Many good men who were truly interested in the troubles of others and wanted to assist them have been so discouraged by the effect of their gifts upon those who received them that they have stopped giving such aid. As a result, when needs are presented to them they are reluctant to help.

These are some of the things that discourage people from being kind. In ancient times in the East, it was a common practice among tribes at war to fill up each other's wells. Every well ruined like this was a public blessing destroyed. Like this, we do wrong to humanity when we allow someone's ungrateful actions to stop the well of kindness in our hearts.

We do serious harm to ourselves and others when we restrain our love and compassion this way. One of the great tasks of Christian living is to keep our hearts gentle and sweet amid all the world's trying experiences. Nothing worse can happen to anyone than to become cold toward human suffering or bitter toward human infirmity and failure.

Jesus is our perfect example. He lived

"WHOM THE LORD LOVETH"

with ingratitude and enmity all His years, but He never became bitter against man. He poured out love, and men rejected it. He helped people in sorest need and distress, and they turned about and joined His enemies. He came to save His nation, and they nailed Him on a cross.

Yet in spite of all this rejection of His love, Jesus never lost a trace of His gentleness and compassion. He was just as ready to help a needy person on the last day of His life as He was the day He set out to begin His public ministry. He healed an enemy the night of His betrayal, and He prayed for the men who were driving the nails through His hands while they fastened Him to His cross.

So love should be our answer to all injury, to all wrong, to all injustice and cruelty, and to all ingratitude. No evil returned for our good should ever discourage us in the doing of good.

Even if our ministry of kindness seems to be an utter failure, our hearts should never lose any of their compassion and yearning. Someone found a fresh-water spring close beside the sea. Twice a day the tides buried it deep under their briny floods. But when the bitter waters rolled out again, the spring was as fresh as before, with no taint of salt in its stream.

This is how it should be with the heart of love. When the tides of unkindness, injustice, or cruelty have swept over it, it should emerge unembittered and unchanged, ready for any new service for which there may be opportunity tomorrow.

That is one of the great lessons Jesus would teach us. We must not allow our spirit to grow bitter when someone abuses our kindness or repays our love with hate. Instead we should take the first opportunity to repeat the kindness and the love, thus overcoming evil with good.

The Master said, **"Love your enemies, bless them that curse you, do good to them that hate you, and pray for them which despitefully use you, and persecute you" (Matthew 5:44).** That is, if someone hates you, he is the very man you are to love. If anyone has used you badly today, he is the very person you need to pray for tonight.

To the carnal man this does not seem possible. No ordinary love can endure such rejection day after day without losing its warmth. No human kindness can meet unkindness continually and yet keep its warmth and generosity undiminished. But the Christian has a power within him that is above his normal humanity. The apostle Paul tells us that **"charity suffereth long, and is kind . . . seeketh not her own, is not easily provoked, thinketh no evil . . . beareth all things . . . endureth all things . . . never faileth" (1 Corinthians 13:4, 5, 7, 8).** Christian love is not an earth-born affection; it is born in heaven, in God's heart. Hence it is immortal, its life is inextinguishable, and it cannot perish. Alfred Austin writes:

> Yet love can last, yet love can last,
> The future be as was the past,
>   And faith and fondness never know
>   The chill of dwindling afterglow,
> If, to familiar hearth there cling
> The virgin freshness of the spring,
>   And April's music still be heard
>   In wooing voice and winning word.
>
> If when autumnal shadows streak
> The furrowed brow, the wrinkled cheek,
>   Devotion deepening to the close,
>   Like fruit that ripens more tender grows;

"Charity Never Faileth"

If, though the leaves of youth and hope
Lie thick on life's declining slope,
    The fond heart, faithful to the last,
    Lingers in love-drifts of the past;
If, with the gravely shortening days
Faith trims the lamp, faith feeds the blaze,
    And reverence, robed in wintry white,
    Sheds fragrance like a summer night—
        Then love can last!

CHAPTER TWENTY

Putting Away Childish Things

> When I look back upon my life nigh spent,
>   Nigh spent, although the stream as yet
>   flows on,
> I more of follies than of sins repent,
>   Less for offense than Love's short
>   comings moan.
> With self, O Father, leave me not alone—
>   Leave not with the beguiler the beguiled;
> Besmirched and ragged, Lord, take back
>   Thine own;
>   A fool I bring Thee to be made a child.
>   —*George MacDonald*

There is a big difference between childlikeness and childishness. The Scriptures commend childlikeness, but childishness is something altogether different. It is one of the things we need to put off and leave behind as we grow into the strength and beauty of Christian maturity.

We can endure childishness in a child. We expect a person to be a baby before he becomes a man. But when childish traits are evident in one who has come to manhood in years, there is no excuse for them. They are blemishes, marks of immaturity. We ought to leave them behind us when we grow into manhood. The testimony of the apostle Paul is *"When I was a child, I spake as a child, I understood as a child, I thought as a child: but when I became a man, I put away childish things"* (1 Corinthians 13:11).

"WHOM THE LORD LOVETH"

Too many people keep their childish ways when they grow up. For example, pouting is a common habit in young children. But every now and then we find full-grown people who have not gotten over the habit of pouting. They are pleasant as long as nothing occurs that injures their self-esteem. But the moment anyone slights them or fails to show proper respect for them, or when others ignore their proposal, they go off in a fit of babyish sulks.

This spectacle is not uncommon among young people in their relations with each other. There are some young people who refuse to share their friends with anyone else. They are like leeches, selfishly fastening their affections to one person and demanding an exclusive right to their affections in return. If the object of their attachment fails to be totally loyal, the doting friend pouts and sulks, whimpering, "You don't care for me anymore!" Such conduct is the token of a sick and unwholesome character.

A true friend is one who is generous and trusting, not exacting and unreasonable in his demands. He is glad to see his friends esteemed and honored by others. Too many people are selfish in their friendships, not only demanding the first place in the affections of their friends, but insisting that they admit no one else to second or third place either.

A selfish person such as this usually will not be a friend; he just wants a friend. Often, such a "friend" will even hinder our spiritual development, demanding affections from us that we should be giving to God and His people. Envy and jealousy are sins and should have no part in the life of a person who claims to be a Christian.

There are other manifestations of feeling and disposition that we should leave behind when we grow up into maturity of life. The apostle Paul names some more sinful qualities that have no rightful place in a Christian life. He instructed the saints at Colosse to put away, **"anger, wrath, malice, blasphemy [and] filthy communication" (Colossians 3:8).**

Instead of these responses, a Christian must allow the Holy Spirit bear His fruit in his life. **"But the fruit of the Spirit is love, joy, peace, longsuffering, gentleness, goodness, faith, meekness, temperance: against**

such there is no law" (Galatians 5:22, 23). These are the character traits of the Christian who has allowed God to do His work in his heart, weeding out the childish and selfish traits of the carnal nature.

Sometimes a childish spirit surfaces in congregational life, when members are chosen for Sunday school offices, or appointed to committees, or given other duties. There are some people who enjoy filling any position of honor or authority but who find it hard to step down gracefully from their position when their term ends. Or it may offend them if someone nominates them for a position, but the congregation chooses someone else to fill it. Some people also take it as a personal offense when the congregation rejects a suggestion they may make in such a meeting.

In any of these cases, there will always be a temptation for ill-will and jealousy, or even pouting, but the mature Christian will not allow these carnal, childish tendencies to rule him. By God's grace he will put these things behind him and give his best service to the church in whatever it calls him to do.

All of these are illustrations of a spirit that is much too common in the world. Such conduct mars the beauty and usefulness of any man. But the Christian needs to overcome these things in his life by the grace of God. It is a sign of carnality within us if we can keep sweet when people are saying complimentary things to us or of us but become discouraged or out of sorts when they ignore us.

The Scriptures teach us to prefer others in honor. When we take this to heart, we will forget ourselves and be happy in the advancement of others.

Let us put away childish things forever. If you find yourself tempted to pout or to be envious or jealous, determine to be Christlike. Will you, by the grace of God, do it?

> I like the man who faces what he must,
> With step triumphant and a heart of cheer;
> Who fights the daily battle without fear;
> Sees his hopes fail, yet keeps unfaltering trust
> That God is God; that somehow, true and just,
> His plans work out for mortals; not a tear
> Is shed when fortune, which the world holds dear,

"WHOM THE LORD LOVETH"

Falls from his grasp; better, with love, a crust
    Than living in dishonor; envies not,
Nor loses faith in man but does his best,
    Nor ever murmurs at his humbler lot,
But, with a smile and words of hope, gives zest
    To every toiler; he alone is great,
      Who by a life heroic conquers fate.